RIVER GANGA
A Cartographic Mystery

River Ganga

A Cartographic Mystery

P.L. MADAN

MANOHAR
2005

First published 2005

© P.L. Madan, 2005

All rights reserved. No part of this publication may be
reproduced or transmitted, in any form or by any means,
without prior permission of the author and the publisher

ISBN 81-7304-637-9

Published by
Ajay Kumar Jain for
Manohar Publishers & Distributors
4753/23 Ansari Road, Daryaganj
New Delhi 110 002

Printed at
Lordson Publishers Pvt Ltd
Delhi 110 007

Distributed in South Asia by
FOUNDATION
B●●KS
4381/4, Ansari Road
Daryaganj, New Delhi 110 002
and its branches at Mumbai, Hyderabad,
Bangalore, Chennai, Kolkata

Contents

List of Maps — 7
Abbreviations — 9
Preface — 11
Acknowledgements — 13

Introduction — 15

1. India in the Western Tradition (BC Era) — 17
2. India in the Western Tradition (Early AC Era – 1500) — 28
3. Lure of the 'Ganga' — 46
4. Changing Perspectives and Perceptions — 71
5. Ultimate Scenario — 102

Postscript — 105

Epilogue — 107

Bibliography — 109

Maps

1.1:	Anaximander (610–546 BC), Map of the World	18
1.2:	Hecataeus (c. 550–480 BC), Map of the World	20
1.3:	Herodotus (c. 484–425 BC), Map of the World	20
1.4:	Eratosthenes (276–195 BC), Map of the World	21
1.5:	Eratosthenes (276–195 BC), 'Dimensions of India'	23
1.6:	Strabo's (AD 18), Map of the World	24
1.7:	Mela's (AD 43), Map of the World	24
1.8:	*Orbis Terrarum* of the Romans by Marcus Vipasanius Agrippa (12 BC)	25
2.1:	TO Map of the World	29
2.2:	Ptolemy, Map of the World	30
3.1:	Detail of Map of Bengal by Joao de Barros (c. 1550)	48
3.2:	*Tabula Asiae X* by Jacobo Gastaldi (1548)	51
3.3:	*Calecut Nuova Tavola* by Jacobo Gastaldi (1548)	52
3.4:	*Second Tavola* by Jacobo Gastaldi (1565)	53
3.5:	Detail of *Orientalis* by Jan Huygen van Linschoten (1596)	56
3.6:	A Description of the East India Company in *The Empire of the Great Mogul* by William Baffin (1619)	58
3.7:	*L'Empire du Grand Mogul* by Nicolas Sanson Abville (1652)	61
3.8:	*Presqu'Inde de L'Inde* by Nicolas Sanson Abville (1652)	62
3.9:	*The Peninsula on this side Ganges* by Robert Morden (1680)	63
3.10:	*Royaume de Grand Mogol* by Pieter van der Aa (1729)	64
3.11.1:	Detail of *Impero del Gran Mogol* (N) by Vincenzo Maria Coronelli (1694)	66
3.11.2:	Detail of *Impero del Gran Mogol* (E) by Vincenzo Maria Coronelli (1694)	67
3.11.3:	Detail of *Impero del Gran Mogol* (S) by Vincenzo Maria Coronelli (1694)	68
4.1:	*Geneologie des Emperus Mogols* by Henri Abraham Chatelain (1699)	73
4.2:	*The West Part of India* by Herman Moll (1712)	74
4.3:	Detail of *Cartes des Cotes de Malabar et de Coromandel* by Guillaume de L'Isle (1722)	75
4.4:	*India Proper* by Herman Moll (1729)	76
4.5:	Detail of *Carte de L'Inde* by Jean Baptiste Bourguignon d'Anville (1752)	77
4.6:	Detail of *Carte Reduite de la Presque Isle de L'Inde* by Jean Nicolas Bellin (1756)	78

4.7.1:	Detail of *Presqu' Isle des Indes Orientales* (NE) by G. Robert de Vaugondy (1758)	79
4.7.2:	Detail of *Presqu' Isle des Indes Orientales* (N-W) by G. Robert de Vaugondy (1758)	80
4.7.3:	Detail of *Presqu' Isle des Indes Orientales* (E) by G. Robert de Vaugondy (1758)	81
4.7.4:	Detail of *Presqu' Isle des Indes Orientales* (S) by G. Robert de Vaugondy (1758)	82
4.7.5:	Detail of *Presqu' Isle des Indes Orientales* (I) by G. Robert de Vaugondy (1758)	83
4.8:	*Carte de L'Indoustan* by Jean Nicolas Bellin (1763)	84
4.9:	*Carte de la Partie Superieure de L'Inde* by Robert Bonne (1771)	85
4.10.1:	Detail of *The East Indes with the Roads* (N) by Thomas Jefferys (1768)	91
4.10.2:	Detail of *The East Indes with the Roads* (E) by Thomas Jefferys (1768)	92
4.10.3:	Detail of *The East Indes with the Roads* (S) by Thomas Jefferys (1768)	93
4.11.1:	Detail of *Hind, Hindoostan or India* (N) by L.S. de la Rochette (1788)	95
4.11.2:	Detail of *Hind, Hindoostan or India* (E) by L.S. de la Rochette (1788)	97
4.11.3:	Detail of *Hind, Hindoostan or India* (S) by L.S. de la Rochette (1788)	99

Abbreviations

Con.	Consultation
Deptt.	Department
Ed.	Editor
Edn.	Edition
E.	East
Govt.	Government
Int.	Introduction
IOLR.	India Office Library & Records
M.	Map
MSS.	Manuscripts
N.	North
N.-E.	North-East
N.-W.	North-West
Pub.	Public
S.	South
T.	Text
T.-M.	Text and Map
Vol.	Volume

Preface

It began long back, when my attention was focused on a map wherein the city of Delhi was shown as a place just north of Daulatabad, hundreds of miles south of its actual position. Looking closely, I was surprised to see that a river 'Ganga' shown flowing in the south-central region of India, and falling into the Bay of Bengal in Orissa. This river was south-west of the great delta of the real Ganga or Ganges, coming from the north-west in Bengal, called Bengala in the map. Two Gangas or Ganges in one map! And this in the map by a well-known map-maker of the time!! This was one of the reasons for my quest for early geographical literature to find out the reasons behind showing Ganga in peninsular India, and the perpetuation of the fallacy for centuries by other respected cartographers as well.

How far this effort, with whatever that could be got from the English renderings or translations of quotes from works in other European languages that have come my way has proved successful in solving the mystery is for the readers to evaluate.

B2/132, Ekta Gardens P.L. MADAN
9, Mother Dairy Road
I.P. Extension
New Delhi 110092

Acknowledgements

Grateful acknowledgements are made for Maps 1.2, 1.7 and 1.8 to Dr R.P. Misra, *Fundamentals of Cartography*, Mysore, 1969; for Maps 1.1, 1.3, 1.4 and 1.6 with permission from J.M. Dent & Sons Ltd., Publishers, *Atlas of Ancient Classical Geography*, London, 1952; Map 3.1, gratefully taken from J.J. Campos, *History of the Portuguese in Bengal*, published by Butterworth & Co., Calcutta, 1919; and the rest gratefully taken from Susan Gole, *A Series of Early Printed Maps of India in Facsimile*, New Delhi, 1984; except for Maps 1.5 and 2.1 which are visualized by the author himself.

P.L. MADAN

Introduction

The western perception of India has varied widely since antiquity. Early Egyptians and Babylonians had a vague idea about the region; Greeks saw the changes more apparent; geographical perspectives and perceptions changed rapidly; science of cartography swiftly advanced; means of collecting empirical carto-geographical data multiplied rapidly; map-makers were busy.

Many inaccuracies or fallacies crept in the early stages of map-making, some inevitable, others not so inevitable.

Map-makers carried on with these inaccuracies not for years or decades, but for centuries. This was done not only by casual map-makers, but even by renowned, judicious, scientific cartographers honoured by their governments and the world renowned geographers, even though Empirical carto-geographical data was close at hand.

Nobody seemingly dared to pick it up for centuries.

Why?

Would the maps and the map-literature produced during this long period reveal the mystery behind this phenomenon?

B2/132, Ekta Gardens P.L. MADAN
9, Mother Dairy Road
I.P. Extension
New Delhi 110092

CHAPTER 1

India in the Western Tradition (BC Era)

Assyriologists, including Dr Saycee and archaeologists are of the opinion that the highly developed ancient civilization of India was, in the third millennium BC, in maritime contact with its counterpart, the highly civilized peoples of the Euro-Asian region of ancient Sumer (modern Iraq) and Egypt.[1] Initially India is believed to have reached the western waters coasting all the way. With the mastering of the monsoon winds, these voyages became more frequent and the 'open sea navigation' got a boost. Indian faces soon became more familiar in the marketplaces of Egypt and Sumer. Later, small Indian settlements in some port-towns also came up. The local people began observing the Indians from close quarters. Naturally, person-to-person contacts and obvious enquiries by the locals brought the two civilizations culturally closer. This interaction went on for centuries, and eventually, India became a 'next-door neighbour' to them. They became more aware of each other's society and culture, and thus gradually began to understand each other's psyche. By this time, the Greeks had advanced, conscious of the progress made by their 'neighbours', the Babylonians and Egyptians, who were enjoying the fruits of 'trade' with India. They were aware of the existence of India, and had a faint idea of it being somewhere in the far East.

How did the heavy logs from India, found in the ruins of Babylonian temples, find their way there in 3000 BC?[2] Who suggested their use? Who selected them? are some of the questions that come to mind. The first question may not be relevant to us here but the others may prove very relevant.

We may speculate that Indians could have been 'helping' the Sumerians materially, since trade concepts were not much developed then. The early known quest for India was started by the Pharaohs of Egypt in 1492 BC.[3] By the Homeric age, around 850 BC, the entire Western world was perhaps aware of India. The Greeks surely heard the noises made by the Babylonians and Egyptians. Not much later, the Greeks were also using articles made in India. But what did India look like? What was the shape and size of India in the perceptions of the 'neighbours', the Babylonians and Egyptians, were hearing and talking about India much earlier than the Greeks? Answers to such questions have not come through clearly because no 'map-illustration' or even a 'graphic diagramme' made in the remote past depicting India's 'face', if at all it was prepared, has survived the ravages of time. This is despite the fact that the art and skill of map-making was already well developed in these civilizations by that time.

By about 600 BC, the Greeks had overtaken their 'neighbours', and marched ahead. The city of Miletus in Greece had already become famous in the West for geographical studies and cosmological speculations.[4] It had produced scholars in almost every field of knowledge, especially history, geography, cosmology, and natural philosophy. Anaximander drew the first map of the then known world;[5] Hecataeus wrote the first book on geography; Herodotus is known as the Father of History.

Anaximander (610-546 BC) is said to have travelled a lot, but whether he visited India is not definitely known. His map of the world does not show the true India, but a tiny part of it, known to geographers in those days as 'India', i.e. the region round the river Indus (Map 1.1).

Even though the main mountain ranges of Europe and western Asia are depicted on the map, the mighty Himalayas are nowhere to be seen. Though several places would surely have been known to the geographers of the time, Anaximander marks only one place, Caspapyrus (not conclusively deciphered yet), on the left bank of the river Indus. The river itself is shown flowing in the south-southeast direction, instead of south-southwestward. The coastline of the subcontinent is not shown, except around the place where the river Indus falls into the sea, called Mare Erythraeum (north-western Arabian Sea). The Indus was perhaps considered the western boundary of India. As the region to the east was not known, it was left blank, but was described as 'perpetual sandy desert'.

The first landmark which represented India to the early Westerners was the river Indus. They believed India existed around the river. What was its shape and extent was not known to them. The first attempt in this direction was made by King Darius of Persia.

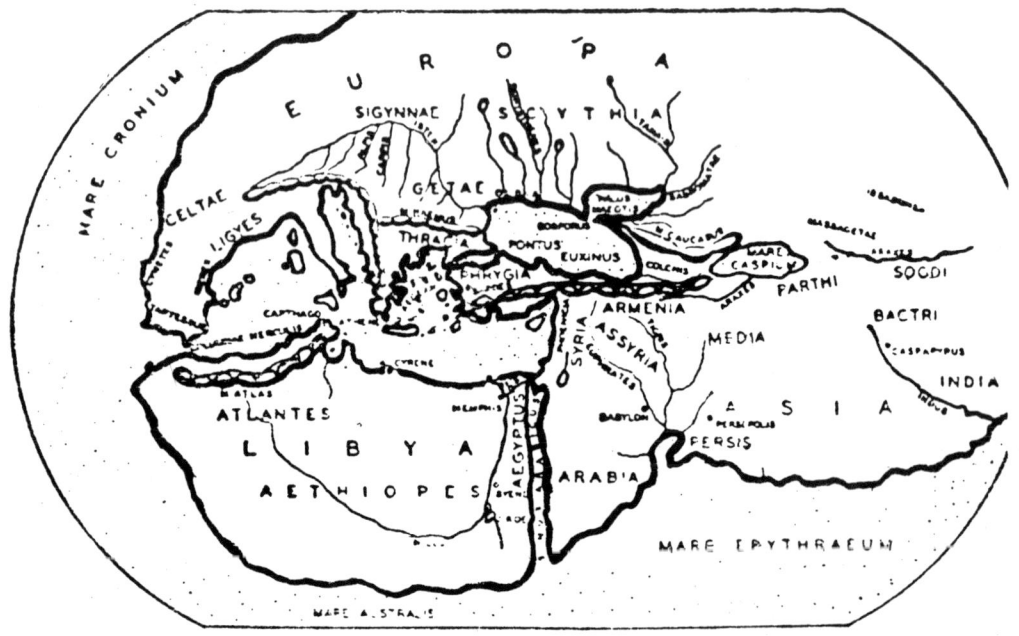

Map 1.1: Anaximander (610-546 BC), Map of the World.

In 515 BC, after the territory around the river Indus was annexed by Darius, Scylax of Caryanda, a Greek officer in his service, was sent to 'India' on a fact finding mission.[6] On return, Scylax submitted his report. His 'report' is even more strange than the already known and familiar image of India, detailed later in the chapter.

Scylax's 'India' is the most remote land to the east of the world. According to him, India, in its north, is thickly populated with fair complexioned but strange-looking people. Some of them are agriculturists and others are nomads living in the northern desert areas. Since India was paying enormous tribute in gold to the Persian king, Scylax says that the huge amount of gold comes from the great anthills found in Indian deserts. In the south of the country live people almost as black as Ethiopeans of northeast Africa with whom the Persians were quite familiar with. An interesting aspect of the report is the inclusion of many fabulous stories about 'India' and 'Indians' in a 'factual' report. One such fanciful story, describes some Indians' as having enormous feet which they use as umbrellas while squatting on the ground.[7] About geographical information, Scylax is all mixed up about geography, about the directions and the distances. And since he did not leave the river Indus to move east into the unknown, to the West, 'India' remained where it was and what it was! But there is no doubt, that Scylax's 'report' aroused Western interest in the geography of India.

It may be remembered that this is the period when the map-makers of the time, influenced by the fabulous stories about India in circulation, and the interest taken by the rulers and the masses alike in Asia in general and India in particular, took their art of map-making more seriously, and the first world map, illustrating the then known world, came about in the form of a Babylonian clay map (*c.* 500 BC).[8]

In 501 BC Hecataeus (550–480 BC), also of Miletus, wrote the first book on geography.[9] He was perhaps not aware of Scylax's voyage down the Indus. He believed the earth to be circular, not spherical, and surrounded by a continuous belt of oceans, with Greece at the centre. In his map (Map 1.2) Hecataeus shows the Indus River flowing from the west to east, and meeting the circular ocean below the Caspean Sea, which is also seen as an opening in the ocean. Ganges was, perhaps, not known to the Greeks at that time.

Another scholar from the same centre of geographical studies, Miletus, was Herodotus.[10] He, like Anaximander, had travelled extensively, but to where all is not precisely known. He also had drawn a map of the world in 450 BC (Map 1.3), and is said to be the first person to describe his geographical views, contained in the *History*. Much of his description of the physical features of India is borrowed from Hecataeus.[11] In the map of the world, Herodotus places India in the eastern-most part of the then known world. He shows the Indus as flowing south-southeastward; and beyond India is endless desert. He divides the Indians into various groups having similar customs and traditions and who speak similar language. He seems to be aware of the 'report' of Scylax. Like him, Herodotus also speaks of fair Aryans in the north and black nomadic barbarians in the south. Herodotus accepted and repeated the fabulous and incredible stories about gold-digging ants which the people in the West were already aware of through the works of earlier writers.

About half a century later, Ctesias of Cnidus severely criticized Herodotus.[12] In his *Indica*, 400 BC, he tried to correct Herodotus on many observations about the East. Although

Map 1.2: Hecataeus (*c.* 550–480 BC), Map of the World.

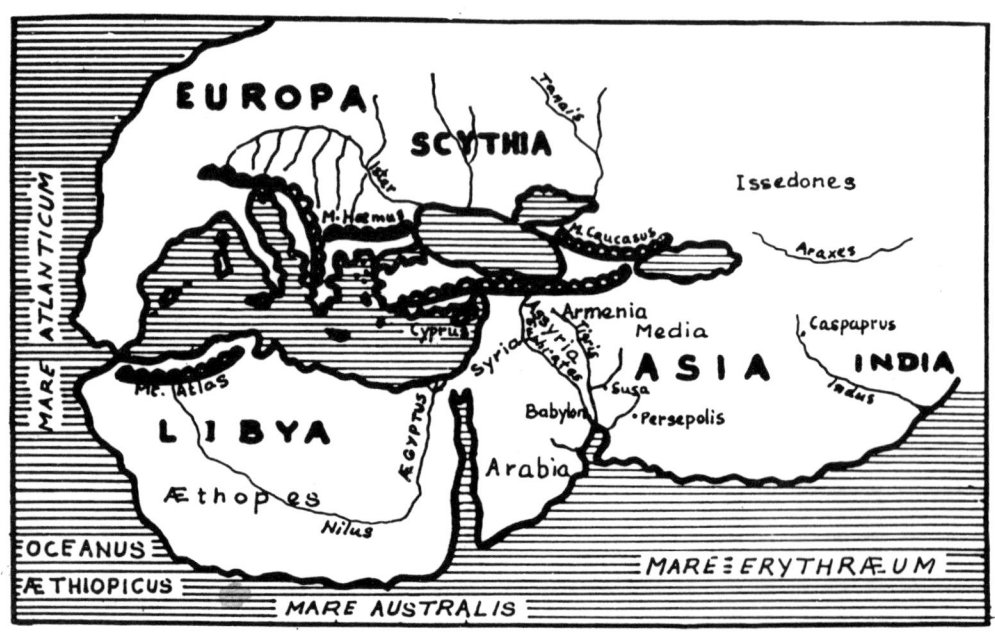

Map 1.3: Herodotus (450 BC), Map of the World.

he was the first author to produce a separate work on India, he was less factual than Herodotus. To the already known fanciful view about India, Ctesias added his own fantastic and imaginary stories. To the grossly exaggerated size of India, 'ten-times larger that the sun' Ctesias which himself felt while in India, and imaginary descriptions of Indian animals and monsters, and a host of other fanciful stories, fables and marvels were added the legends and romances of Alexander's campaigns into India which had become popular by then. This trend continued through Pliny to the writers of the Middle Ages (AD 300-1300) who added their own fanciful ideas.[13]

In the meanwhile, the mathematics, astronomy, and the physical sciences advanced tremendously, which helped cartographers. Mathematical theories like Pythagorus have made the depiction of spherical earth on plain surface, like a map, simpler.

The first person to use scientific and mathematical approach to cartography was Dicaearchus (350-290 BC).[14] A disciple of Aristotle, he pointed the necessity of using an 'orienting line' on the world map that made coordination of various places easier and more accurate. He preferred the line to pass through Gibraltar and Rhodes islands, and to extend it as far as Persia.[15] Later, Erastothenes (276-195 BC) improved upon the idea by using more lines parallel to one another in his map of the world (Map 1.4). But he did not space them at equal intervals. He also devised a way to represent the spherical earth on a plain surface by extending two parallels eastward, one passing through Gibraltar and the Caspean Sea, and the other through Egypt and southern India. He also fixed a zero meridian passing through the Nile River, but starting from the mouth of the river Don. This map is, perhaps, the first to show the river Ganges. It is shown issuing out of the Mons Taurus (Himalaya mountain) from a place east of the Indus, flowing eastward, parallel to tie mountain to its south, and falling into the sea just south of the Mons Taurus at the end of the world.

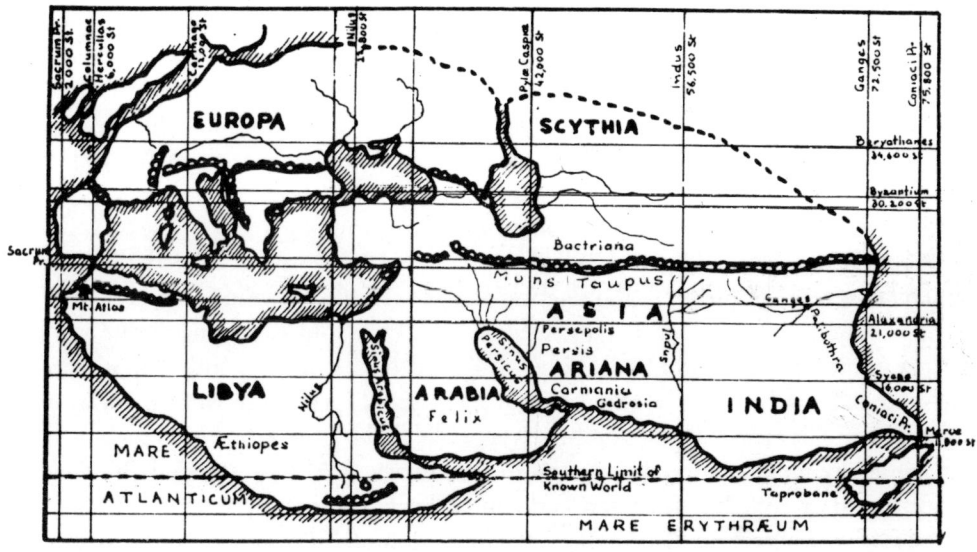

Map 1.4: Eratosthenes (276-195 BC), Map of the World.

During 326-234 BC, Alexander of Macedonia was occupied with the campaign in northwestern India. This conquest brought the regions of East Europe, Asia Minor and India 'geographically' close to one another. But it was only after the death of Alexander in 323 BC that the factual geographical details of the Indian phase of his expedition were collated and written about. It was left to these later writers to improve upon them and write factual histories.[16] Even after the death of Alexander, the Greeks maintained their contacts with India. Seleucus Nikator, the successful successor to Alexander appointed Megasthenes as his ambassador to the court of Mauryan ruler Chandragupta,[17] in the early fourth century BC (303-299 BC).

Megasthenes, in his writings and reports clearly stated, 'India's boundaries, its general configuration, its precise dimensions, both in length and breadth, its physical features, . . . While at the Court, he gathered material from his personal observations as well as by inquiry, and compiled, it in a book viz., *Indika*.'[18] The original work is not extant now. The subsequent Greek writers extensively quoted him, and it is from these that we have our present knowledge about Megasthenes. Dr Schwanbeck has collated all the fragments pertaining to him, and a fairly readable account is available now. 'The works of historians of Alexander and the account of Megasthenes set the image of India for the Greek world.'[19]

The death of Alexander in 323 BC triggered a scholarly debate over his exploits, resulting in histories based on facts,[20] which lasted till the ushering in of the Christian era.

There were many writers who accompanied Alexander,[21] and others came on the scene after his death. Out of those who were eyewitness to Alexander's campaigns, only two could impress the then elite who were interested in such accounts. These were the two who, in fact, gave the then cartographers enough empirical cartographic data to base their maps upon. One of these was Aristobulus, an architect, and the other was Ptolemy, a student of military operations and founder of the famous Egyptian dynasty named after him. The works or memoirs of all these who accompanied Alexander are not extant now,[22] but their views are preserved in the works of a few later writers, more famous of whom are Strabo, Pliny, and Arrian. The accounts of the writers referred to above significantly enlarged the available material for the 'factual' histories that came soon after, although the originals of these early 'factual' histories are lost. Their data, however, are preserved in Arrian's *Indica* (*c.* AD 150).[23]

By this time Alexandria had replaced Miletus as the centre of geographical studies in the West. Alexandria was founded by Alexander of Macedonia as the capital of Hellenic Egypt in 332 BC. The city was completed in the reign of Ptolemy II, Philadelphus (285-247 BC). The famous library there contained, at that time, about 7,00,000 books according to one account, but another version puts the number at about 4,00,000. In the nearby temple of Serapis also were deposited about 2,00,000 books as part of the great library. These were given by Mark Antony as gift to Cleopatra. These volumes were collected by the kings of Pergamus.[24]

A huge geographical material collected in the library at Alexandria after the death of Alexander. The data available there was augmented by Eratosthenes, being the librarian at Alexandria from *c.* 234 to 196 BC, by collecting Greek classical knowledge about geographical theory.[25] Although the three of his books of *Geographica* are not extant, his thoughts are preserved in Strabo's work, along with the criticisms of them by Hipparchus. Like the Pythagorians, Eratosthenes also believed in a spherical earth which he measured and divided into zones. By measuring the shadow of the sun at Alexandria and Syene, he estimated the circumference of the earth, to be 24,662 miles, a few hundred miles short of the correct figure. In his effort to delineate the known portion of the world on a plane surface, Eratosthenes took the island of Rhodes as his centre and calculated distances along the two lines which intersected there.[26] He started with the Ganges at the earlier end and proceeded westward identifying the place names and the main physical features along the line. He plotted and delineated the broad features of the world taking the two parallels and the meridian as his main coordinates. He also computed the shape, size, and placement of India.[27] To have a reasonably correct shape of India, he made a quadrilateral projection (Map 1.5). Through this dimensional projection, one can see clearly the peninsular shape of south India. But the latitudinal extension of Asia more than longitudinal width in the map cannot be missed, His sense of direction and the lengths of the two main rivers, Indus and the Ganges, were somewhat distorted, perhaps due to his efforts to fit in his coordinated calculations. McCrindle writes that it was Eratosthenes who 'raised geography to the rank of science, by collecting its facts hitherto scattered and disjointed, and arranging them in a system framed on scientific principles'.[28] 'It was in the library of Alexandria that Eratosthenes wrote the work which began the real mapping of the globe with the lines of latitude and longitude.'[29] '... Eratosthenes' map which ranges from Ultima Thule in the far north to Arabia Deserta and the Indian limits, carry the record to the point where the line contact between geography and ancient history occurs.'[30]

Eratosthenes was the first map giving details of India as a landmass. He was the first map-maker to visualize the eastern and the southern extents of India; and the first to mark the river Ganges, as far as possible, at its proper place on a map. Though the placement is not accurate, it gives a sufficiently correct idea to the people so far as the eastern 'boundary' of

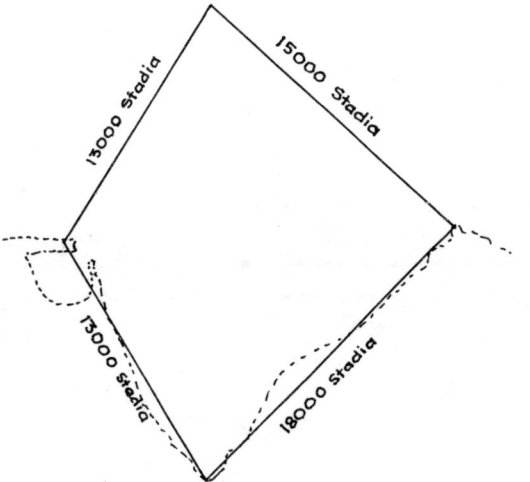

Map 1.5: According to Eratosthenes (276-195 BC), 'Dimensions of India'.

India' is concerned. But the sources of the Ganges and its upper course, especially through the Himalaya, was enmeshed with controversies which erupted later, and remained for centuries. Strabo (63 BC-AD 21) (Map 1.6) and Mela (AD 43) (Map 1.7) also showed Ganges in their maps, but had no idea of the surrounding region, and the direction of the flow of the river.

The work of Eratosthenes was theoretically improved upon by Hipparchus (180-125 BC)[31] by proposing a scheme of 360° of latitude and longitude. He also compiled a comprehensive list of latitudes and longitudes of many places. As there were no instruments at that time to easily calculate longitude of a place, important suggestions of Hipparchus regarding the construction of a map, in the absence of required astronomical data, remained on paper only. He himself could not prove the utility of his theory of map-making by

Map 1.6: Strabo's (AD 18) Map of the World.

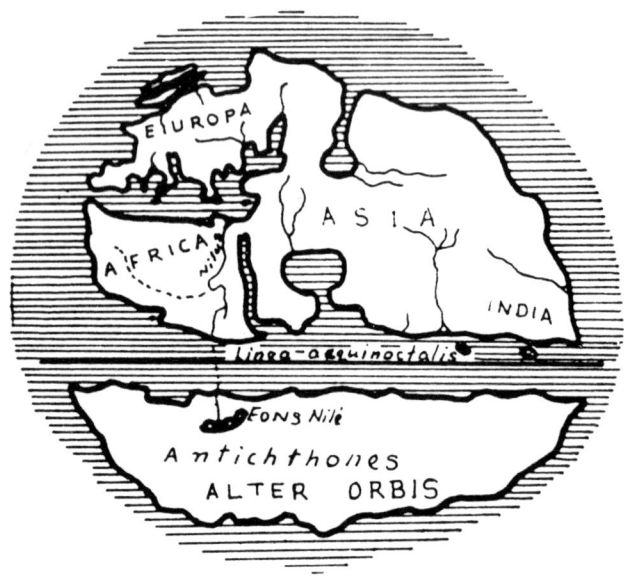

Map 1.7: Mela's (AD 43) Map of the World.

preparing a map himself. All the same, Hipparchus is credited with laying the foundation of the scientific approach to practical cartography, which centuries later were worked upon by Ptolemy.[32]

In the closing years of the BC era, another map which gave a little twist to Megasthenes' map of India, and adjusted itself with a *mappae-mundi*, was drawn in 20 BC by Marcus Vipasanius Agrippa (63-12 BC). The map is called the *Orbis Terrarum* (Map 1.8) of the Romans.[33] After the death of Agrippa, the map was exhibited at the Campus Martius in Rome. Copies of this map were prepared for displaying at important cities of the empire, but unfortunately they are all now lost.[34] The *Orbis Terrarum* or 'the survey of the world' is based only on road-surveys and place-names and other features are not astronomically determined. It is a circular map with Greece at the centre, and is east oriented. In the Asian region, the Indian landmass is shown as triangular in form, with the peninsula of India missing, and the rivers Indus and Ganges, forming the two sides of the triangle. The coastline joining the delta regions of both these rivers, almost in a straight line, constitutes the third line of the triangle. The map does not seem to follow any known rule of projection, nor any constant uniform scale, and no proper directions have been used to determine distances and directions between places.

But one thing is clear—the eastern boundary of India, in the European conception, was represented by the Ganges. This has come to stay in the minds of map-makers. People in general, and map-makers in particular, were eager to know the details about this river which, they knew, was part of the Indian psyche, and a part of the life of every Indian from birth till death, that the waters of the Ganges were regarded by the Indians as sacred. The Europeans

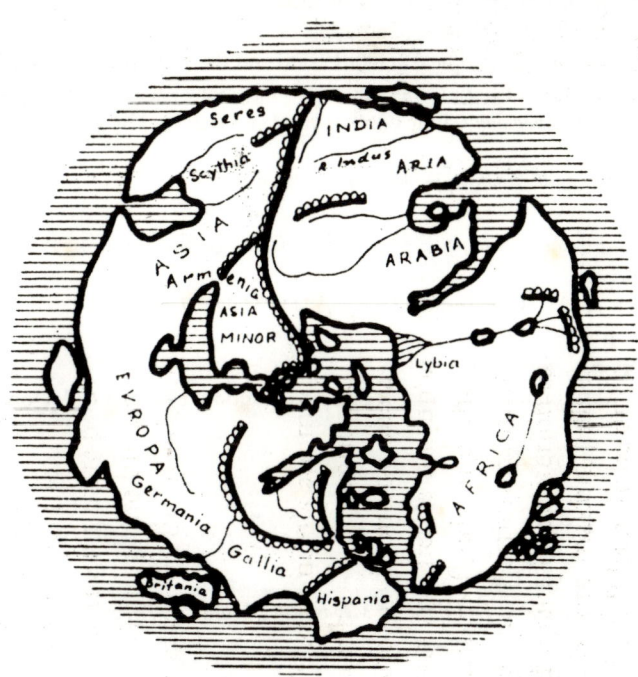

Map 1.8: *Orbis Terrarum* of the Romans by Marcus Vipasanius Agrippa (12 BC).

knew about the many legends and myths associated with it and its source since antiquity. The European intelligentsia was even speculating about its origin. During second century AD, even Ptolemy in his *Geographia* speculated that the Ganges issued out from a place enclosed between the mountains which separate India and Tibet.[35] Agrippa's map (Map 1.8) is perhaps, the only map which illustrated the collective Greek cartographic wisdom of the BC era, and passed it on to the Christian era. Ptolemy later picked up the thread later and laid the foundation of modern scientific cartography.

During the latter half of the BC era, many Western writers like Pliny and Megasthenes wrote about the social, cultural, and religious beliefs of Indians, along with related empirical geographical data through their writings. For many centuries later, then did why the Western cartographers fail to assimilate their own classical geographical knowledge into their cartographic vision of India till the middle of the second century of the Christian era? Why did they continue with the distortions when their 'scientific' maps were being produced later, even when the explicit empirical data was available to them since the Middle Ages? Why did they incorporate into their maps many of the proven geographical fallacies despite the cartographic progress and the rapidity with which they achieved excellence in geography, is something to ponder about.

NOTES

1. Hibbert Lectures, 1887, 'Origin and Growth of Religion among the Babylonians', quoted in R.K. Mukherjee, *A History of Indian Shipping*, 2nd edn., 1957, p. 60.
2. Charles Verlinden, 'Indian Ocean: The Ancient Period and the Middle Ages', in Satish Chandra (ed.), *Indian Ocean Explorations in History, Commerce and Politics*, New Delhi, 1987, p. 30.
3. Leo Bagrow, *History of Cartography* (Eng. edn.), revised and enlarged by R.K. Skelton, London, 1964, pp. 31-2.
4. R.P. Misra, *Fundamentals of Cartography*, Mysore, 1969, p. 22.
5. Leo Bagrow, op. cit., p. 33.
6. Donald F. Lach, *Asia in the Making of Europe*, 3 vols., Chicago and London, 1965-93, vol. I, pp. 5-6.
7. Ibid., p. 6.
8. Leo Bagrow, op. cit., p. 31; R.V. Tooley, *Map and Map Makers*, London, 1970, p. 3.
9. R.V. Tooley, ibid., p. 4.
10. Donald F. Lach, op. cit., vol. I, p. 6.
11. M. Cary and E.H. Warmington, *The Ancient Explorers*, London, 1929, pp. 6-7; Donald F. Lach, op. cit., vol. I, p. 6.
12. Donald F. Lach, op. cit., vol. I, p. 7.
13. Ibid., p. 7.
14. Leo Bagrow, op. cit., p. 33.
15. Ibid., p. 33.
16. Donald F. Lach, op. cit., vol. I, p. 8.
17. Ibid., p. 9; N.S. Kalota, *India as Described by Megasthenes*, Delhi, 1978, p. 19.
18. N.S. Kalota, op. cit., p. 20.
19. Donald F. Lach, op. cit., vol. I, p. 9.
20. Ibid., p. 8.

21. Ibid., p. 8.
22. Ibid., p. 8.
23. Ibid., p. 8.
24. *Atlas of Ancient Classical Geography*, London: J.M. Dent & Sons, 1852, p. 87.
25. James Oliver Thomson, *History of Ancient Geography*, Cambridge, 1948, pp. 21-2; Donald F. Lach, op. cit., vol. I, p. 10.
26. Donald F. Lach, ibid., vol. I, p. 10.
27. Ibid., p.11.
28. J.W. McCrindle, 'Introduction', in *Ancient India as Described in Classical Literature*, Westminster, 1901, p. xi.
29. 'Introduction', in *Atlas of Ancient Classical Geography*, op. cit., p. v.
30. Ibid., p. v.
31. R.P. Misra, op. cit., p. 27.
32. R.V. Tooley, op. cit., p. 5; R.P. Misra, op. cit., p. 4.
33. R.P. Misra, op. cit., p. 27.
34. Leo Bagrow, op. cit., p. 37.
35. R.H. Philimore, *Historical Records of the Survey of India*, 5 vols., Dehra Dun, 1945-68, vol. I, p. 71.

CHAPTER 2

India in the Western Tradition (Early AC Era–1500)

In the initial stages of the Christian era, two distinct cartographic currents were flowing in the world. These were deeply influenced respectively, by the two great religions of the world, Islam and Christianity. Initially their influence, however, was not interacting cartographically in any way. The cartographic movement was carried away by practical Islamic religious thoughts and practices like finding coordinates of places not for building mosques but prayers facing Mecca, for following trade routes, etc.; whereas the other was moving from the secular Greeks, the Romans, to the Portuguese, and the other European nations, finally culminating in what is generally known as 'European Thought'. Both these movements had, however, a significant common link, though the 'link' influenced them differently, and strangely enough, after a gap of more than a millennium.

This common 'link' came about on the scene in the second century AD Klaudios Ptolemonios (AD 87-150, active between AD 127-50), a Greek resident of Alexandria in Egypt and better known as Ptolemy, developed a revolutionary concept of map-making. His theory is detailed in the famous work *Geographia* (discussed later) which he wrote in second century AD. A thread from this scientific piece of work was picked up in the seventh century by trader-navigators and map-makers of the Middle East, better known in the cartographic parlance as the Islamic cartographers, or Arab cartographers.[1]

Due to their early trade contacts with the East and the West and their navigational skills and astronomical interests, the Arabs were expected to know and contribute much in the fields of sea-charting and consequently the terrestrial mapping.

Between the end of the BC era and the Arab cartographers of the seventh century AD, there came a period when almost everything was stagnant in the cartographic world,[2] except the consolidation and compilation of the ideas already prevailing in the Western world. The Romans came to the centrestage and began directing the cartographic activities, though with little success. Rome also replaced Greece as the centre of political authority and 'hegemony of Rome over Egypt and the Red Sea littoral' came about. This made possible the emergence of new activities and contacts in the Mediterranean region and the East.[3]

The Roman cartographers took advantage of the political calm prevailing in the region and began the work of consolidation and compilation of geographical data from the classical Greek period, and the information available before the European Renaissance.[4] They took these compilations as their groundwork, and began preparing their own maps from them.

These compilations were later used by the Latin and Arab map-makers and geographers as well. Even Ptolemy based much of his work on them. The Romans did not contribute much in the sphere of the cartography of the Asian region, more particularly of the Indian subcontinent. Their cartographic perception of India and its geography was vague.

Upon the dissolution of the Roman Empire, the Arabs became the 'intellectual heirs of the Greeks'[5] in the seventh century. The centre of learning shifted from Alexandria to Baghdad and Damascus. It was at these centres that much advancement was made in geographical, mathematical and astronomical speculations. It goes to the credit of these developments that the European geographical and cosmological held on through a period of stagnation and later picked up the threads for further progress. The Arabs maintained their hold over cartographic thoughts till about the twelfth century.

In the last years of the Roman Empire direct relations between the East and the West gradually ceased. But individual merchants and traders from the West still continued, on rare occasions, to find their way eastward. Cosmos Indicopleustes decided to take the sea-route to India, reached the western coast of the peninsula, stayed there for some time, and resided at Ceylon before moving on. From the information gathered during his travels, he prepared a geographical treatise called *Universal Christian Topography* (AD 540).[6] He is critical of the Greeks, but his own compilation is a 'fantastic medley of hard facts and religious theory' about the world's topography.[7] He is not specific about Asia. He advocated the theory of flat earth with Jerusalem, instead of Greece, as the centre.

Near stoppage of trade between the East and the West was followed by the rise of Muslim political power in the seventh century and consequently Arabs took centrestage. During the first Christian millennium, the Bible increasingly became the main source of geographical knowledge. The European writers gradually began to follow the Christian biblical fantasies and ignore the classical delineation of the East.[8]

The most significant contribution to medieval cartography (c. 300-1300) was the development of the 'TO' maps (Map. 2.1), detailed later. These were most popular between

Map 2.1: TO Map of the World.

the eighth and thirteenth centuries when Marco Polo's adventures and his geographical revelations began to dislodge the unempirical geographical ideas. The TO maps were later superimposed with 'climatic' and 'inhabitable zones' theories and subsequently, Ptolemic ideas were added by the Arab cartographers to suit their Islamic conventions and beliefs. The Arab cartographic wave continued till the fourteenth century, after which it was greatly influenced and modified by Marco Polo's thoughts.

Early in the medieval period, geographical ideas in the Muslim world rapidly advanced. There were some European and Muslim traders and travellers to give eyewitness accounts of the geography of India, but Muslim cartographic vision of India remained distorted. Arab cartography took a turn in the ninth century when Muhammad ibn Kathir al-Fargani (d. 830), a geographer, made Ptolemy's *Geographia* (Map 2.2) accessible to the Arabs by translating it into Arabic. He also introduced the concept of climatic zones.[9] From ninth to the thirteenth centuries, Ptolemy's great work was being translated and increasingly adapted by Arab scholars like the Caliph al Mamun, the founder of the 'House of Wisdom', al Khwarizmi in his *Face of the Earth* and Abu Yusuf Yakub. The result, however, was that the 'terrestrial maps' of the Arab scholars showed markedly distorted South Asia. Idrisi, though an Arab scholar, worked for many years at the court of Roger II of Sicily. He, like many other geographers of his time, compiled his own geography, entitled *Book of Roger*. While writing it, he depended largely on Ptolemaic thought prevailing in the Arabic cartographic world,[10] but which had not by then penetrated into European geographical thought. Idrisi's geography is considered a great work by present-day scholars, but it did not attract much attention in his days.

The European cartographic wave, on the other hand, in its beginning in the AD era could be traced to early Roman trade with the East and the interaction with the Indians present at Alexandria and at other trade centres, and the influence of the Indian culture and thought on the West.

Map 2.2. Ptolemy's Map of the World

In the first two centuries of the Christian era, Roman trade with the East flourished. Almost all the trading nations of the time east of Turkey were in contact with Rome; India and China were the most favoured nations. Due to this, geographers of the West had first-hand geographical information from the navigators, traders and even from casual travellers. Alexandria was acting as a storehouse of information as it was one of the major entry points to the West at the time. Ptolemy had also had derived his conception of India from these sources, along with the Greek works of antiquity (Map 2.2).

There was close contact with India at that point of time. Merchants, emissaries, and even slaves from India were seen in almost every important town in Latin Europe.[11] Though Roman institutions were slow in their interaction, the Western intelligentsia of second century, like the Platonists and Manichaeans, were quick to assimilate much of Indian culture. The way for them had opened somewhat early by the historians of Alexander. Clement of Alexandria (d. AD 220) was the first to exhibit any real knowledge Indian philosophy, and to mention the Buddha in his writings. Philosophoumenos (c. AD 230) of Hippolytus, a well-known writer of the early Church, give enough proof of the influence of Indian culture over Roman thought. His work reveals his considerable direct textual knowledge of the great Indian *Maitri Upanishad*, an explanatory treatise of Indian metaphysics in the form of a poetic dialogue.[12] 'Nor is Hippolytus entirely alone.' There are many others in the first three centuries of the Christian era who believed that 'eastern barbarians probably possessed secret ways of attaining a closer and purer knowledge of the divine than was known in the West.'[13] Plotinus (c. AD 204-70) was a great scholar of Indian Upanishads; Yoga doctrine of Patanjali was very popular with the neo-Platonists. Mani, the prophet of Manicheanism had stayed in India for quite some time. He places the Buddha at par with Jesus, Adam, and Zoroaster as the divine emissaries.[14] Indian philosophical thought was so popular and so widespread in the West during the early Christian era that Manichaeanism was proscribed and banned in the Roman Empire during the time of Diocletian, in c. AD 296 by the Byzantine Church;[15] Mention of the Buddha, though denunciated by the Roman Church, can be found in the works of later Roman writers. Strangely enough, in the eleventh century, the name of Buddha was christianised to Josaphat,[16] and the name of a Hindu ascetic Bilahaur, to Barlaam.[17] The legends and fables connected with both of them did not die with the imposition of restrictions by the Church. There were others who were thus converted by the aggressive Christianity. 'The careers of *Barlaam* (*Buddha*) and *Josaphat* (*Bilahaur*) were introduced at an early date into the *Vitae sanctorum*, and Roman martyrology where they still figure today on the date November 27.' The legends of Buddha and Bilahaur became more popular thereafter in the Latin world; these names were added to the repository of the Roman saints in the eleventh century.[18]

India was still considered by the general masses to be too far away from Europe. Factual knowledge, as illustrated by Eratosthenes and Pliny of the BC era, was limited. India was described by the Church and considered by the masses as the 'land of marvels and the habitat of monstrous animals and peoples'. By the third century, information about the East became increasingly more profound and general.[19] Though the people in the West, during Roman times, were interested in Indian philosophy and thought, they did not seem to be interested in India's geography. Their concept of India had not much improved over what it was at the end of the BC era.

Arabs' knowledge, about India was, however, more factual, though it did not encompass a larger horizon than that of their counterparts in Europe. This could be because Ptolemy's views prevailed in the Arab world about a millennium earlier than in Europe.

Traditional depiction of monstrous and fabulous East which was inherited by the geographers and map-makers from the Greeks, was still being assembled and popularized in the third century by Solinus in his work *Collectanea rerum memorabilium*;[20] Augustine included a chapter about the fabulous 'races' in his work *City of God*.[21] Even the writers of early medieval period did not include the classical delineation of the East.

In the fifth century, Martianus Heraclea wrote *Periplus of the Outer Sea*. In this book he stated the eastern boundary of India, though indirectly. He wrote: 'In trans-Gangetic India is the Golden Khersonese (peninsula) and beyond it is the Great gulf, in the middle of which is the frontier between trans-Gangetic India and the Sinai.'[22]

But all these did not have any significant effect on the later medieval commentators who still adhered to the ideas that that prevailed in the earlier medieval ages and also to the earlier mythical fancies, like those of Isidore, and Seville (d. 636). Seville's *Etymologiis* was considered a standard geographical reference work on Asia during this period. In his treatise, Isidore's main stance is his reliance upon the Bible and some of the 'Latin purveyors of mythology'. It is during this period that numerous geographical beliefs like a flat earth, inherited from antiquity, were given the authority of the scriptures by Augustine, and Isidore the original exponents of the idea.[23] Both exponents of Christianity began experssing on geographical theories citing Bible as authority. The factual information that the early medieval commentators derived from the classical writers is often distorted or made 'so confused with later myths as to be unrecognizable'. These later myths were both literary and geographical.

The maps, till the Middle Ages, were not entirely based on classical empirical data, and even did not show true orientation and topography. They, however, contained geographical fantasies and unaligned data. May be this was because of lack of scientific cartographic innovations available or invented till then. But in the competitive market, many of the map-makers announced their maps to be based on newly added empirical data.

The Middle Ages saw the myths incorporated in the popular literature since very early days and forcefully re-expressed by Ctesias and the exponents of the 'romances of Alexander', and those who gave these myths and fables the authority of the scriptures from Bible, including the geographical phantacies, forcefully propagated at that time by Christian zealots, finally amalgamated them with biblical allegories. Even the myths, like India being the land of monsters and mystics lying somewhere in the east, are slowly and gradually enmeshed in the popular thinking of the people in Europe during the Middle Ages. Asia is generally considered as the source of the entire Paradise, and its rivers like the Indus, Ganges, Nile, and Euphrates are thought to be originating from a 'common source in the Garden of Eden'.[24] These ambiguities continued to retain their hold over the popular imagination for centuries, after when Marco Polo visits and describes the 'terrestrial Paradise' to the people who are continued to be influenced by the already popular literary and cartographic thought even during the

Crusading era. The geographical myths in the Middle Ages are now being more forcefully perpetuated as the map-makers are more in demand in the later Middle Ages, in the Rennaissance period, and in the Age of Discovery that followed, because the lure of the geographical myths are becoming more and more attractive with the new discoveries.

These legends or literary stories were not directly connected with the perpetuation of geographical myths about India among the Europeans. But since the Latin world was full of such myth and fables,[25] they nonetheless, make us believe that the Latin world was prone to accepting the geographical myths or fantasies also as gospel truths and, thus, helping to perpetuate them for centuries, even when empirical details were always for them to check up. One such effort was made in the mid-fourteenth century by a Spanish Franciscan through his popular *Book of Knowledge of all the Kingdoms, Lands, and Lordships in the World*. This book reveals that the author had a reasonably accurate geographical knowledge of the East, including India. But his observations 'combine, at times bewilderingly, the factual with the fanciful'.[26] His accurate naming of the eastern cities, information about lands and sea routes and general knowledge of the country earned him the respect of the readers. Such works though few, were there in this period.

However, contrary to the above, in the West 'In the millennium after Ptolemy, three legends of European origin nourished and elaborated the view of the fabulous East'. These legends revolved round the saga of St. Thomas, the Apostle of India. These were; (i) existence of a cult of the apostle in India, (ii) the growth of the Prester John legend, and (iii) existence of a powerful Christian ruler to the east of the Muslim world. These came about, and became popular although the empirical writers and map-makers were competing hard with their empirical informations to change the West's concept of India of old myths, both literary and geographical.

Broadly stating, one of the best well-known literary myths in the West, though not directly connected with Indian geography, is that of imaginary king Prester John of the 'crusades'. 'From the middle of the twelfth century to the beginning of the fourteenth century at least, the belief was common place in Europe that somewhere in India (perhaps including Africa in this concept) a pious and fabulously wealthy (Christian) king ruled who had waged successful wars against the Medes and Persians and who might be induced, if he could be reached, to take up the sword against the Saracens.'[27] Throughout the thirteenth century, travellers, including Marco Polo looked for this king but in vain. In the succeeding century, Odoric Pordenone is the last writer who thinks that Prester John's kingdom is somewhere in Asia. Thereafter, the legend's locale shifts from India to Africa. Why? Could it be the apprehension in the minds of those floating such myths and fantasies of being exposed by truly empirical information with unrefutable proofs by those who would be able to go to the Indian Ocean littorals in the east somewhat freely and in greater number, in the later years?

However, many of the Indian literary fables and motifs are incorporated into European imaginative literature since a very early date (some of them have already been described earlier). These, of course, migrated through the Muslim world, and in various languages, like the story of the migration of the *Panchatantra*, a well-known collection of Indian tales. Its route to the West lay through Syria. It was first translated into Syriac in the sixth century, then into Arabic in the eighth century, and into Hebrew in the twelfth century. Again, John of Capua translated it into Latin around 1263-78. Other Indian tales also entered Latin literature in a similar fashion.[27] People of the Latin world were fond of fables and legends and loved to recite them at every opportune moment till about the Middle Ages. Latin has an abundance of such legends. Many tales from the *Jatakas* are incorporated therein. Well-known legends and parables relating to the lives of Barlaam and Josaphat, Lain versions of Indian tales, migrated to Europe via the Levant. The parables and legends of Buddha were originally taken from the *Bhagwan Bodhisattvascha*. These were translated into Latin in the ninth century by Anastasius Bibliothecarius. In the tenth century, St. Euthyme d'Hagiorite translated it into Greek. These parables and legends are so popular in Europe that they were repeated for centuries, some in abridged forms. In the thirteenth century, Vincent of Beauvais incorporated the abstracts of these tales in his work *Speculum historiale*, and Jacobus de Voragine did the same in his *Golden Legend*. Even today fables of Barlaam and Josaphat are found in the Roman history of martyrs and other related works.[28] Starngely, these Indian legends and parables which travelled to the West and remained popular with the masses, and ideas of India and Buddhism which they reflect, are now completely in oblivion as these have, since long, been 'christianized,' and the characters, Barlaam and Josaphat are now examplars of Christian saintly figures.[29] Their 'origin' came to be known long after the opening of the sea route to India in the fifteenth century, and began to be appreciated by some of the Western writers thereafter, although these legends, even now, are quoted as 'literary dramatic themes' and 'historical sources' in the West.[30]

While many of the early works incorporating such legends are generally classified as 'travel accounts', these are not even remotely connected with travel literature. These accounts make references to India only to describe old stories of the 'dog-headed' people, monsters, mystics, and fantastic animals. The great 'empirical' travel literature in Europe is believed to have emerged with the travels of Marco Polo in the late thirteenth century which, incidently, became the source of a fantastic geographical fallacy on the Indian cartographic scenario (discussed later). One such travel scout account of early thirteenth century (1245 or 1257) commented upon by C. Langlois, in French, includes a long poem entitled *L'Image du monde*, a general practice in those days. The poem gives a fantastic and, no doubt, highly imaginary description of India and its people, 'India has two summers and two winters each year, but the climate is so mild that plants stay green at all seasons. Located near Ceylon (Taprobane or Sri Lanka), India is the country of gold, precious stones, spices, and coconuts. It is divided into twenty-four heavily populated regions inhabited in parts, at least, by horned pygmies, who live in groups and become old in seven years. These pygmies inhabit the country of white pepper. Beasts and men with six toes or fingers are not oddities. The Brahmans of India commit suicide, by throwing themselves into a fire; others eat their old parents to do them honour.'[31]

By looking at such European perception of India and its people during the Middle Ages, it appears that neither the works of antiquity nor the accounts of Arab and Jewish travellers, with empirical data, influenced the popular image of India. This was perhaps, because the people had by than imbibed the spirit of the Crusades, and had evolved their own evangelistic notions and reasons of India. It is interesting when one looks at the image of India with monsters roaming about and the Christian missionaries eager to teach them Christianity under the influence of the Prester John legend. This idea did prevail in some quarters of Europe. The proof can be found in the painted tympanum of the central interior portal of the cathedral of Vezelay, completed around the mid-twelfth century, wherein a Christian teacher, reported to be the Christ, is depicted as addressing and instructing 'cynocephalic Indians and other monstrous peoples'.[32] It is surprising that despite European travellers and merchants visiting India, no important and realistic account of the region came out in medieval Europe after the work of Cosmos, referred to earlier. And even the Eastern monsters and other legends appearing in European literary world were 'Christianized' into local literary and religious idioms, like the cases of Barlaam and Josaphat. Europe is thus being provided with nothing 'more than a sketchy and distorted picture of India known to Alexander . . .'.

While literary writers and religious zealots could easily distort through enchanting stories which were easy to concoct than to draw in figures on geographical maps to that effect and 'Christianize' the literary myths and legends, the then map-makers, could not do the same to geographical fantasies to such an extent. They, however, did not have any option but to likewise "reflect a scriptural and fanciful view of the world'; and myths and vagaries continued to be drawn on maps right through the eighteenth and early nineteenth centuries, which the later writers and map-makers could present before the people as the 'eye witness' accounts of European travellers. This aggressive posture of Christianity was visible in the activities of the early missionaries.

Portugal witnessed political turmoil and religious persecutions in the last decades of the thirteenth century and the beginning of the fourteenth century, covering the period before and during the Crusades. In general the Portuguese supported the actions of the Church and played an active part in the Crusades. In 1319, they formed their own crusading militia known as the order of Christ. They were engaged in the propagation of Christianity, battling of infidels, and the conversion of heathens to 'bring light to people living in Pagan darkness'. On board the first vessels that left for Malabar in India, ostensibly for trading purposes, missionaries and secular priests were seen in good number. These people later fought and died side by side along with the *fidalgos* for the sake of the faith.[33]

During the fifteenth century, when Europe's geographical knowledge about India was limited, Portugal launched its path breaking voyage eastwards. Significantly, the Pope had blessed Portugal's missionary intentions by putting the evangelic jurisdiction of the entire East in its charge. In 1534, the Pope gave the right of royal patronage to the Portuguese king; successive papal briefs confirmed this right. These gave the crown the authority to nominate all bishops, dignitaries and parish priests in the territories in the East. In return, Portugal promised to safeguard the Church's interests and propagate the faith by supporting the clergy and the religious institutions. Thus, 'mission and colonial expansion grew together'; and 'defence of the *padroado* was almost a patriotic duty'.[35] The masses hesitated to go against the ideas enshrined in these understandings and the authority vested in the State and its secular and ecclesiastical officials. To them, these views were almost gospel. On the other hand, the missionaries who visited the East were the main purveyors in Europe of information about non-commercial and non-political aspects of life in Asia, including India. Their view, naturally, had all the biases of ecclesiastical commentators, historians and even travel-account writers.

In AD 1240, Mongol chief Chenghis Khan, shocked the east European Christian rulers by invading them. Reconciliation with this new situation took about a quarter of a century. In 1264, Mongol hegemony in western China, south of the Wall, was extended by Kublai Khan, who made 'Cambaluc' (Peking) his capital.

In the mid-thirteenth century, when Arab cartographic thought was on the decline and Ptolemaic ideas had not taken Europe by storm, land-routes from Europe to Mongolia were reopened as a result of the Mongol incursions into Europe. This was followed by the extension of Mongolian hegemony into China, as we have seen. In 1260, two Venetian merchants, Nicolo and Maffeo (Polo brothers) left Crimea. They were the first Latin Europeans to visit Kublai Khan at Cambaluc. They were closely questioned by him, but were unable to satisfy the Khan's curiosity. They were then sent back to the Pope as his emissaries. After some years, both the Polos were appointed by the Pope as Apostolic delegates to the Khan's court. On this journey in 1271, Nocolo's son Marco and two other Dominican friars accompanied them. The friars were to represent Western learning at Cambaluc.

While living in China under the patronage of Kublai Khan, the then ruler of China, Marco Polo had the official permission to move about all over the country, including the remotes areas. Marco took down notes on topography and the people for the Khan. It was perhaps during one such trip to the farthest remote areas that Marco described the existence of mythical 'lake Chiamay' in the southwest of China, or somewhere in the southeast of Tibet, or in the region northeast of Bengal or Assam. It was 'for the first time in history Europe possessed a detailed narrative about China and its neighbours based upon more than hearsay and speculation'.[36] His book, *The Description of the World* (1298-9) was written not by Marco Polo but by Rustichello, a fellow prisoner in Genoa after both were captured in a naval battle in September 1298. Rustichello's original version was entitled *Livre de diversities* written in Old French. He was a writer of popular romances. But some scholars argue that Marco Polo dictated his story as a romance 'for the enjoyment of his contemporaries'.[37] This narrative account gave rise to the second fallacy on the Indian segment of Asian cartography, detailed later.

In the fourteenth century, geographical information of a more realistic nature derived from Ptolemaic literature of the Arabs writers, the experiences of Muslim traders and travellers going to the East, and the new terrestrial maps based on empirical information and technique of the portolan map-makers —who had by then begun to show the interiors of the countries in the East as well—was being increasingly seen in Europe. This made the serious scholars in geography, cartography, and the general intelligentsia to suspect and feel the necessity of looking afresh into the geographical conceptions and ideas together with maps being prepared at the time. Their suspicion was genuine as they felt that the maps were not being made according to scientific principles and empirical data, as understood by them, and thus were faulty and vague, if not entirely mythical.[38] This mental conflict went on for centuries, as we shall see in the later chapters, shaping and reshaping perceptions of India. The Arab mapmakers' geographical knowledge of the interiors of India, as revealed in their maps, however, was extremely meager, contrary to their geographical treatises.

By now, in most of the medieval maps the Ganges had established itself as the 'known world's eastern boundary', and the Sahara desert its southern frontier. The entire inhabited world is shown as an island surrounded by a universal sea. The maps that have survived, like the Beatus charts of the eighth century, are east oriented. On the other hand, Bede and some other writers are closer to Greek views, but their conceptions of the physical world held little attraction for the medieval map-makers, more especially those of the era before Marco Polo.[39]

Production of 'true' maps based on portolan techniques used for modified depiction of the known world gradually began to take shape. The growing tendency to base maps on empirical data, and on travel accounts of the like of Marco Polo and his successor travellers could now be seen coming up in Europe. The earliest map of this nature, which is extant, is the Lauratian portolan, drawn in 1351. Herein, the Indian peninsular form began to emerge. Another 'true map' of the portolan nature is dated 1375 and is called the 'Catalan Atlas'. Prepared for Charles V of France, this is the work of Abraham Cresques, a Jew from Majorca. It is now preserved in the Bibliotheque Nationale in Paris.[40] As against the Ptolemaic work coming out of Arabic world, the emergence of peninsular India, in much clearer form, or even 'truer' in form than that shown even in the Lauratian portolan, are the main developments so far as the Indian cartography is concerned. No map in 'truer' form was even made in a century hence. The cities are marked in the interior of the map as per the understanding or the data available to the cartographer from the travel narratives. These may not be in the accurate positions, but are still more or less in the correct places.

This was the cartographic scenario in Europe in the fourteenth and fifteenth centuries when Ptolemy's *Geographia* was published a few years later. The effect was stunning. Almost immediately, the work's defects became apparent. But the map-makers took up the new innovations in earnest, and in good spirit. At first, they had very little to base their criticism of the emerging geographical and cartographical theories and perceptions, except their general belief in the old classical ideas and religious conceptions, which were to them much stronger.

The exhaustive gazetteer of places, arranged region-wise with their latitude and longitude, is considered to be the main chapter of Ptolemy's text. His division of the globe into 360° of latitude and longitude, and his deduction of the length of a degree at equator or of a meridian, and his calculation of the circumference of the earth were the bases on which his theory depended. He also suggested a method of adjusting the length of a degree of longitude for any given latitude. He also explained how to construct a network or 'grid' of parallels and meridians for maps to be drawn on a conical projection.

The second part of Plolemy's treatise is the collection of maps—a world map and regional maps. It is still doubtful, and not yet conclusively settled, whether the maps were drawn by Ptolemy himself and were part of the original work. He, however, implied that any intelligent reader using the guidelines contained in the text could prepare his own maps.[41] It may be noted that the maps which reached fifteenth-century Europe—whoever drew them and whenever these were made—'were based on his coordinates and drawn in his projection'. And because of this, all the defects and merits of Ptolemy's theory with minor differences,—depending on each writer's interpretations or personal knowledge of the subject—appear on the maps drawn by others (Map 2.2).

The most interesting part of the cartographic scenario, from both theoretical and practical points of view in Europe, was that the renowned scholars of geography and cartography during this period had no 'reliable criteria for criticising Ptolemy, just as they had none for criticising Marco Polo'.[42] Ptolemy's works were not intellectually incompatible and seemed beyond controversial possibilities. His maps, or the maps based on his theory, seemed superior and more scientific than the medieval *mappa-mundi* and even the portolans. His use of coordinates seemed much more logical and revolutionary to what they had heard or seen till then. His was major step forward in the science of map-making.[43] This can be illustrated by what Cardinal Pierre d'Ally wrote in early fifteenth century, detailed in the chapter.

The effect of *Geographia* on the thinking and working of even prominent map-makers could be illustrated by an example. French Cardinal Pierre d'Ailly, a renowned geographical theorist of his time, wrote his *Imago Mundi* in 1410. D'Ailly was very much impressed by the geographical thoughts of Bacon of the thirteenth century. He copied the geographical thoughts of Bacon from his *Opus Majus* of 1264, almost word for word, in his *Imago Mundi*.[44] This was before when the *Geographia* of Ptolemy in Latin came before the Europeans. D'Ailly was, at first, a staunch follower of classical thought, including the theory of zones or climates. He believed in the exaggerated east-west extent of Asia and the proportion of land to sea in the area of the globe. He knew many of the prominent Arab geographical scholars of his time. In spite of all his acquaintances with the geographical scholars, he had fixed ideas. He strongly believed that the ancients had a better knowledge of geography and cosmography than the fifteenth century European scholars. He was 'the herald of a new and exciting series of classical recoveries, and of geographical works based on their inspirations'.[45] His *Imago Mundi* was printed at Louvain in about 1483. His thoughts influenced Columbus very much. In his personal copy, Columbus had, in his own hand, made many annotations in the margins. This copy is now preserved in Columbina at Seville.[46] His *Imago Mundi*, however, his spherical maps of inhabitable zones do not show the delineation of terrestrial boundaries of continents and the topographical features, and hence, are of no use in our present study. Soon after when D'Ailly came across the Latin version of Ptolemy's *Geographia*, just after three years of his first publication, he, in 1413 wrote his second work, the *Compendium Cosmographiae*, in which he summarized the ideas of Ptolemy, as he could understand them. Within this short period, after going through the *Geographia*, he changed his views on many points. In the *Imago Mundi* D'Ailly had described an open Indian ocean, but now he agreed to with Ptolemy. Even the famous Humanist and Geographer of his times, Pope Pius II, was greatly impressed and his *Historia rerum ubique gestarum* was considered by the cartographers, as a 'digest' of Ptolemy.

By going through the details of what Ptolemy had left for us, we know that he amassed a huge collection of astronomical and other scientific and technical data for making a map of the known world and many regional maps; we know he had compiled a gazetteer of coordinates for which he had consulted a number of periploi; he studied the theoretical aspects of cartography of projections, especially of conical projection which he preferred; we also are made to believe that he had interacted with navigators, traders and travellers passing through Alexandria while returning from the East; he also would have, we have reasons to surmise, surely discussed his favourite subject of cartography, its various constituents, with the Indian traders, navigators and others to collect first-hand knowledge also. It is highly unlikely that he kept his mission secret from them all. There is every possibility that while discussing about the Indian subcontinent, surely this must have been his favourite area of investigation, being conscious of its social, economical, cultural and also geographical importance since antiquity to all the Mediterranean and the Asia Minor littorals, he must have also been told of the southward peninsular projection. Surely, either he did not agree to their views or did not discuss the delineation of the Indian coast-line. Since he compiled the lists of coordinates of places region-wise, his expert eyes could have immediately noticed the almost near uniformity of the latitudinal or parallel readings or values of places on the coasts in the list, indicating thereby the almost straight east-west projection of the coastline, but, it is strange that the apparent discrepancy between the near uniformity of his latitudes of the coordinates and verbal description to him of the peninsular shape, so described by almost everyone to him, did not register on him. He could never have been so adamant as not to see the reason behind the eye-witness's account, more especially of the navigators who always update their portolans on actual observations at sea, on the spot. It seems, he did not discuss with others his objectives and his own periploe.

Another point that emerges out of the whole confusion is that Ptolemy did not prepare any map of the world himself, and, again, if he had, he did not discuss his own map with any east-west navigator because of the reasons, discussed above. It is apparent from the points already raised that Ptolemy did not cross-check his thesis with any one, and did not illustrate his own theory graphically on paper, or did not put into practice his own advice or suggestion to others about map-making. But it cannot be denied that he dominated the cartographic world for centuries to come.

The fifteenth-century Ptolemaic geographers' perception of India was that it encompasses only the territory between the Indus and the Ganges, the locale of the old kingdom of 'Eli', The Persians, who live adjacent to northern India, call it, in Barros' words by 'its proper name, Indostan'. The whole of India, the Portuguese chronicler observes, is bounded by the Indus, the Ganges, the Indian Ocean, and the great mountains of the north called 'Imaos' by Ptolemy.[47]

A significant change in the whole cartogeographic scenario came about at this time. An important travel account appeared in Europe. This was by a Venetian, Nicolo de Conti, who, after remaining 25 years in the East, returned to his native country in 1441. A merchant traveller, he came into contact with a Near Eastern delegate to the Ecumenical Council of Florence held in Tuscany, Italy, in 1441. On his return, he was very closely questioned by the papal secretary and renowned humanist Poggio Bracciolini, about the 'Christian Indies' consisting of Ethiopia, India, and Cathay (China).[48] The contention, it seems, was to locate old 'Prester John' kingdom. Conti's itinerary took him farther than any former European ever travelled, beyond the island of Taprobane (Sri Lanka). He voyaged up the Ganges for three months and described the voyage and the places around the river in detail. Married to a woman of Indian origin, his account presents Indian manners and customs in a lucid way;

and contain notable similarities with Megasthenes' account particularly the motion that Indians unlike the Europeans, are relatively free from disease and pestilence, etc.'His account is remarkably free of the European popular beliefs about India—its insular character, its dog-headed peoples, its demons and monsters—with which Megasthenes' story had been embellished over the centuries.'[49]

From 1431 to 1447, Poggio gathered material for his own work, *Historia de varietate fortunae*, which was published in four volumes. Book IV contained information about India, based principally, but not exclusively, on his interrogation of Conti.

Conti's account supplied enough empirical geographical material to the map-makers of fifteenth century for charting India's land and waterways, just as the most critical student of Ptolemy, the Pope Pius II (in office, 1458-64), better known to the cartographers of the day as Aeneos Sylvius Piccolomini was supplied material for his work *Historia rerum ubique gestarum* (1461).[50]

On the other hand, there were other renowned geographers and map-makers who, it seems, deliberately ignored the empirical information available to them and prepared their maps, depending chiefly on Ptolemy, Marco Polo, together with accounts of India from Pliny, Solinius, and Isidore of Seville, thus perpetuating the geographical and literary myths.[51] Other prominent cartographers of the time were Henricus Mertellus, a German who lived and worked in Italy, the well-known globe maker Martin Behaim (d. 1506), and to some extent Pierre d'Ailly (1350-1420).

There were few maps and geographical accounts during the fourteenth and fifteenth centuries that were able to bring together the materials of the classical nature and empirical data regarding the East gathered from the accounts of Marco Polo and his precursors and successors. But strangely enough, 'much that was, fabulous, particularly about India, continued to detract from the significant advances that had been made in the acquisition of a truer picture'.[52]

The invention of the printing press in the fifteenth century and the subsequent revolution that took place in printing and bookmaking technologies gave chance to the urban middle class and the gentry throughout Europe to study geography and understand the travel accounts of Portuguese explorations and discoveries that were in full swing at the time. As the book trade was already secularized in the previous century, this century saw a rapid mushrooming of professional copy-houses in many parts of Europe which turned out a wide variety of manuscript books. This century also witnessed many paper mills which came to Europe from the East; its early development was in Spain during the twelfth century. The printing and manufacture of books was accelerated by the invention of the movable type, also in the fifteenth century. The mechanical printing processes spread out extensively in western Europe. This enabled book- and map-makers to disseminate their carto-geographical knowledge of the discoveries of Asia, including India more speedily. The presses in Germany, Italy, France, and Spain were more active in bringing latest discoveries to their people. For instance, Nicolo de Conti's travel accounts of 1447 or 1448 was published in 1461 by Poggio Bracciolini, and by Pope Pius II (in office, 1458-64), better known as Aeneas Sylvius Piccolomini, also in 1461. Fra Mauro in *c.*1459 brought out Conti's map.

Although, as already stated, the book trade was secularized in the fourteenth century, intensive campaigns by the Church in the fifteenth century saw a large number of religious works of many varieties. In the sixteenth century, presses in many cities were producing Latin works for international consumption as well. With growing literacy in western Europe in this century, all the major centres of book production, like Rome, Paris and Lyons in France, London in England, Cologne, Stressburg and Augsburg in Germany, Lisbon (after mid-century) and Coimbra Portugal (Madrid came very late in the century), Antwerp in Netherlands, and Seville in Spain all began producing books about discoveries as well. Annual book fairs for international consumption were being regularly held at Frankfurt, Mainz, and Lyons.

Portuguese book-makers were, however, working under harsh secrecy laws of their government. During the latter half of the sixteenth century, with the growing demand for books on discoveries along with the maps of the newly discovered regions, the Portuguese began circumventing the secrecy laws. On the other hand, cartographers, map-makers, and printers began liaising within their trade circle for rapidly getting and disseminating carto-geographical information for boosting their business. A variety of map producers began increasingly printing maps of the East from the manuscript maps of the Portuguese sources of the last century. Copies from the existing world maps from various sources were being added to the large number of travel accounts coming up, and were being included in the already well-known atlases. Portuguese cartographers working or living overseas were in great demand. They began selling their services and their information about the new world to foreign governments and entrepreneurs who were not so resourceful so as to get carto-geographic information by direct means. 'Portuguese students and Professors at the college of Sainte-Barbe in Paris relayed information on the discoveries of their compatriots to interested French geographers and cosmographers. To Dieppe (Norman town), Portuguese captains carried information on geography and navigation, and other well-guarded secrets of the Portuguese admiralty. Joao Ofonso emigrated from Portugal to France around 1528, and in La Rochelle, where he settled, he prepared charts and cartographic sketches for the French expeditions.'[53] It is already well known that before 1540 almost all the maps prepared in France were based on the Portuguese portalans.

This brief survey of the activities of the press during the fifteenth and sixteenth centuries in Europe indicates that gathering of carto-geographical information about the newly discovered countries and its dissemination throughout Europe was not much of a problem for the people in the business.

Apart from Conti, other travellers of the fifteenth century were Pero de Covilha, a Portuguese, in 1487 and Girolamo da Santo Stefano, a Genoese who travelled to India and the Far East around 1493. The last of the known independent travellers before the opening of the sea route was an Italian named Ludovico Varthema. It was in Rome in the year 1510 that his famous work *Itinerary* was published. The geographical information about India that filtered out in the fifteenth century to the readers was much less than what it was in the previous century. Some writers tried to reconcile the 'geographical learning of the past with the practical experiences of more recent voyagers'. 'The European image of Asia (including

India) in the fifteenth century was still compounded of a mixture of fact, theory and myth. Uncritical use of the available materials from the classical heritage sometimes even increased the number of fanciful notions. At the same time, some of the myths and legends that came in the Middle Ages continued to enjoy respectability, long after other vestiges of medieval life had been discarded.'[54]

From the sixteenth to the eighteenth centuries, the Portuguese controlled maritime trade on the Indian Ocean, though the period also saw succession of other 'foreign' periods like the Dutch period, the English period, and in between was a period of internal European conflict effecting the maritime activity in the Indian Ocean.

In the sixteenth century, the geographical perception of India formed from the early classical literature of antiquity, the Bible and the Western writers was still being guided by myths, fables and geographical fantasies, even though significant advances were made in the acquisition of materials projecting a true picture of India and its geography. This was discernible when Ramusio's great collection of travel accounts appeared in 1550 (detailed later). Printed maps, prepared generally from the manuscripts of Portuguese cartographers and existing world maps of varied origins began to come up in great numbers, illustrating literary and travel accounts. Ramusio's account, however, added another fanciful geographical absurdity to the already confused state of European geographical perception of the Indian subcontinent—the river 'Ganga' in the southern peninsula, where there was none by this name and description. This was the result of Ramusio's 'adoption' of Barros' description of the 'Ganga', and his inclusion of it in his maps.

If we examine an early map at a much later stage in time, say in a later century, as we are doing now in the twenty-first century, inaccuracies are bound to be seen, especially in the regions for which no proper geographical information was available for the then mapmakers to work upon. But when we know that empirical data is available to the cartographers, but it is ignored, deliberately or otherwise, and it is announced that the map is 'based on new information' or 'revised with additions and corrections', then the situation becomes ambiguous. It becomes all the more perplexing when such irregularities are perpetuated by almost all the map-makers not for a few years but for centuries together; one is then bound to look for reasons elsewhere.

In the ancient maps, as we have seen, the river Ganges was considered as the eastern boundary of India, and later, of the then known world. While delineating it, every mapmaker and geographical writer from Eratosthenes onwards must have speculated over the place of origin of the river. Since the coming into vogue of Ptolemaic theory of scientific map-making, this aspect was deliberated and speculated upon by the serious cartographers. Another reason for it getting attention was the 'legends of mystery' surrounding the source of this venerated and holy river of Asia. The Ganges invited comments from historians and geographers alike since the early Greek times. Ptolemy in the second century commented that the ancients knew as little of it as of the origin of the Nile River of Egypt.[55] We know that Ptolemy's *Geographia* came to Europe in the fifteenth century. Between the fifteenth and seventeenth centuries, hundreds of maps were made by various cartographers. Since these were based mostly on Ptolemy's ideas, their depiction of the source of the Ganges did not differ much from Ptolemy's. In the post-Ptolemaic period, every map-maker used his own judgement. Curiously enough, in the fifteenth century itself, the geography of the source of the great river attained another dimension. The great Persian historian of Timur, by the name of Schereseddin, stirred the imagination of many map-makers by speculating that this holy river of India sprang from a place 15 miles above the straits of Kupela (the gorge above Rishikesh, north of Hardwar) through a mighty rock cut in the shape of a cow.[56] This statement took an interesting turn in the subsequent years (discussed in later chapters).

The earliest of the maps of the sixteenth century which illustrate the mental conflict of fifteenth-century map-makers is by Juan de la Cosa, a former pilot of Columbus. Other well-known maps of the century are the *King-Hamy-Huntington Chart* (1502), manuscript map of Alberto Cantino of the same period, the world map by Contarini (1506), and various editions, both manuscript and printed, of Ptolemy by renowned cartographers such as John Ruysch (1508), Martin Waldseemuller (1470-1518), Lopo Homem (1519-54), and Sebastian Munster's various editions of his own *Geographia* (1540-52). Though famous in the cartographic world for their individual qualities, these maps did not show details of the interior of India.

Although the map-makers were enchanted by Ptolemy's thesis, certain events of the late-fifteenth and sixteenth centuries made dents in these beliefs. The significant events that gave a shattering blow to Ptolemaic influences and completely changed his 'world' were: (i) Dias' (1487) and Vasco da Gama's (1499) voyages round the southern tip of the African continent, the Cape of Good Hope, to the Indian Ocean, and the sailing round the globe by Magellan (1522), and del Cano, the captain of the only surviving ship *Victoria* of Magellan's fleet. This revealed to the world, for the first time, the immense size of the Pacific Ocean, thus unsettling the easterly extent of Asia's land mass as calculated by Ptolemy. These two events did give a jolt to the Ptolemaic ideas, but did not diminish the popularity of *Geographia*, or its hold over the minds of serious map-makers who still carried out experiments based on his innovations.

Magellan's voyage blew another myth—that the Ganges was the eastern boundary of India and beyond that it is mostly 'uninhabitable desert'.

NOTES

1. Leo Bagrow, *History of Cartography* (Eng. edn.), revised and enlarged by R.K. Skelton, London, 1964, p. 53.
2. R.P. Misra, *Fundamentals of Cartography*, Mysore, 1969, p. 25.
3. Donald F. Lach, *Asia in the Making of Europe*, 3 vols., Chicago and London, 1965-93, p. 12.
4. R.V. Tooley, *Map and Map-Makers*, London, 1970, p. 9.
5. Ibid., p. 9.
6. Donald F. Lach, op. cit., p. 22.
7. Ibid., p. 22.
8. Ibid., p. 22.
9. Ibid., p. 53.
10. J.H. Parry, *The Age of Reconnaissance*, London, 1963, p. 11.

11. James Oliver Thomson, *History of Ancient Geography*, Cambridge, 1948, p. 349.
12. Ibid., p. 18.
13. Ibid., p.18.
14. Ibid., p. 19.
15. Ibid., p. 19.
16. Donald F. Lach, op. cit., 27 (n. 80), quoted from Paul Peeters, 'La Premiere traduction latine de "Barlaam et Josaph" et son original grec', in *Analecta Bollandiana*, XLIX (1931), pp. 276-312; P. Peeters, *Recherches d'histoire et de philologie orientales*, I, p. 19, n. 1; J. Jacobs, *Barlaam and Josaphat*, London, 1896, facing p. 10.
17. Donald F. Lach, op. cit., p. 27, n. 80.
18. Ibid., p. 19.
19. Ibid., p. 19.
20. Ibid., p. 22.
21. Ibid., p. 22.
22. Paul Wheatley, *The Golden Khersonese: Studies in the Historical Geography of the Malay Peninsula Before A.D. 1500*, Kuala Lumpur, 1961, p. 135.
23. Donald F. Lach, op. cit., p. 23.
24. Ibid., p. 23.
25. Ibid., pp. 27-8.
26. Ibid., quoted from C. Markham (trans.), *Book of Knowledge* . . . , Ser. II. London: Hakluyt Society Publications, 1912, pp. x-xi.
27. *A History of Sanskrit Literature*, Oxford, 1928, pp. 357-65.
28. Donald F. Lach, op. cit., p. 27; A. Berriedale Keith, op. cit., pp. 357-65.
29. Ibid., p. 27.
30. Ibid., p. 27.
31. Ibid., p. 29.
32. Ibid., p. 30; quoted from J.F. Filliozat, 'Les premieres etapes de l'indianisme,' in *Bulletin de L'Association Guillaume Bude*, III, 1953, p. 81; Emile Male, *L'Art religieux du XIIe siecle en France*, Paris, 1922, pp. 329-30.
33. Donald F. Lach, op. cit., p. 229.
34. Mira Mascarenhas, 'The Church in Eighteenth Century Goa', in Teotonic R. de Souza (ed.), *Essays in Goan History*, New Delhi, 1989, p. 94. Historical Archives of Goa, Ms. 1437, fls. 138 V-141.
35. Mira Mascrenhas, op. cit., p. 94, quoted from M. Saldanha, 'A primeira imprensa em Goa', *Boletim Instituto Vasco da Gama*, 1956, vol. I, pp. 355-6; see also L. Ratus (ed.), *Catholic India*, New Delhi, 1982, p. 4.
36. Donald F. Lach, op. cit., p. 35; quoted from the John A. Scott (trans.), and L. Olschki (revised), *Marco Polo's Asia: An Introduction to His 'Description of the World' Called 'Il Milione'*, Berkeley, 1960.
37. Ibid., p. 35.
38. Ibid., p. 66.
39. C.R. Beazley, *The Dawn of Modern Geography*, London, 1897, I, pp. 375-91.
40. Donald F. Lach, op. cit., pp. 66-7.
41. J.H. Parry, op. cit., p. 11.
42. Ibid., p. 13.
43. Ibid., p. 13.
44. J.H. Parry, op. cit., p. 9.
45. Ibid., p. 9.
46. Ibid., p. 9.
47. Donald F. Lach, op. cit., pp. 340-1.

48. M. Rogers, *The Travels of the Infante Dom Pedro*, Cambridge, Massachusetts, 1961, pp. 65-7.
49. Donald F. Lach, op. cit., p. 62.
50. Ibid., pp. 70-1.
51. Ibid., p. 70.
52. Ibid., p. 222.
53. Ibid., p. 71.
54. Ibid., pp. 85-6.
55. R.H. Phillimore, op. cit., vol. I, p. 71.
56. William Herbert, *A Geographical Illustration of the Map of India* (2nd edn.), 1759, p. 21.

CHAPTER 3

Lure of the 'Ganga'

The sixteenth-century Europe saw some significant manuscript narratives on India, mostly by Portuguese and Spanish writers, along with a flood of travel literature by others. Tome Pires wrote *Suma Oriental* between 1512 and 1515; the *Book* by Duarte Barbosa came out in 1518; *Historia general de las Indias* by Francisco Lopez de Gomara in 1552, and three volumes of *Historia de descobrimento e conquista da India pelos Portuezes,* by Fernao Lopes de Castenheda (1500-59) in 1551-2; subsequent four volumes came out of the press in 1554. Joao de Barros (*c.* 1496-1570) published his first work in 1552. Barros, the greatest Portuguese historian and chronicler of the century,[1] made use of the accounts of Tom Pires, Domingo Paes, and Fernao Nuniz in his chronicles. For his geographical locations he was careful enough to accept the evidence, oral or written, chiefly of sailors, pilots and navigators who had been in the Eastern waters. He continually revised and expanded as new information came his way. His work is one of the classics of Portuguese literature and of European historiography.[2] For his remarks on India, he collected Persian, Arabic, and Indian manuscripts, and got them translated, even if he had to purchase educated slaves for getting this done. According to his own statement, he used the information judiciously in order to produce a balanced narrative without 'too much of any one thing'.[3] But according to some writers, Barros' maps and writings on the geography of India disseminated one of the most inaccurate and perplexing information regarding Indian geography—the depiction of a mythical river 'Ganga' in peninsular India where there was actually none by this name and description.

Because of it being inordinately detailed and exhaustive, Barros' chronicle was not republished in Portugal in the sixteenth century. The Europeans, however, continued to be informed of his ideas about India through another channel—Ramusio incorporated six chapters, translated into Italian, from Barros' *Decadas da Asia* in his 1554 edition of the first volume of *Delle navigationi et Viaggi.* By the latter half of the sixteenth century entire Europe was aware of the great work of Barros. Venice honoured him by placing his port portrait in praise the great litterateur of the age, and Pope Pius IV placed another of his portraits next to the statue of Ptolemy in the Vatican, a symbol of Barros-Church relations.

Portugal's close relations with the Church since the thirteenth century, the obligations under *Padroado* and the later the papal bulls, Barros' reputation as a historian and chronicler, his official position together with his standing as a geographer and map-maker and his being the son of a *fidalgo* all led his books to be received with great appreciation by the people and the scholars. Even later writers like Ramusio, another giant in the field, respected Barros' geographical knowledge about the East, particularly India because of his well-known methodology of checking, counter-checking and constantly updating his geographical writings as and when fresh information poured in. Almost all the writers of the period were apprehensive and sceptical about criticizing his views and information unless they had authentic empirical proofs to counter them. His statements were taken as correct, and his 'Ganga', therefore, continued to be seen flowing in peninsular India in the later maps by future cartographers of Europe. Strangely, no empirical information seems to have come Barros' way throughout his long distinguished career of more than three decades to cause him to revise his views in the *Casa da India*!

William Herbert, in his English rendering of D'Anville's memoir of his famous map, Carte de L'Inde (1752) echoes this sentiment:

Behind these mountains (Western Ghats), as were told by Barros, sprang two rivers, Crusar and Benhorz; the first to the Northward of the other; these rivers uniting in the environs of Andanagar (Ahmadnagar) ...form the great river Ganga.... The want of intelligence concerning a great space of country, leaves without any account of the course of this river, till we take it up again towards the place where it divides into several channels, to get into the Ganges and the sea.[4]

This unambiguous statement was enough from the mighty pen of Barros to influence even the radically thinking later mapmakers to carry the river on future maps for centuries.

Barros' map of Bengal (*c*. 1550) (Map 3.1) is, perhaps, the earliest map showing the imaginary river Ganga in peninsular India. The map is east oriented and gives details of the delta region of the Ganges. No longitudes are marked. It covers the territories between 21° and 27° latitude, from Orissa in the west to the Arracan in the east. River Ganga is shown entering Orissa and meeting the western channel of the Ganges' delta, known as Hooghly.

Barros' another inaccuracy was the emergence of river Brahmputra, which he calls as the Caor river, from the lake 'Chiamay' located in Assam.[5] This lake, it may be recalled, was first mentioned by Marco Polo in 1298-9. This later turned out to be another geographical myth adopted by many European map-makers.

In the latter half of the sixteenth century, another of the Europe's greatest historians, chroniclers, map-makers and a well-known humanist of his times appears on the scene. The author of a travel narrative as well, Giovanni Battista Ramusio (*c*. 1485-1557) collected his narratives mainly from the Venetian printers and a group of Venetian literati with whom he appears to have come in contact quite early in his literary career.

The first volume, which mainly included new information on Asia, was published in 1550. It was republished with amendments in 1554, 1563, 1588, 1606, and 1613 (this edition contains six chapters from Barros' vol. I). In his introduction, Ramusio states that the purpose in compiling the work is to collect materials and maps of Africa and the East, including India, and 'presumably many of the other notions about these regions inherited from the writers of antiquity and the Middle Ages'.[6] Ramusio also adds three double-paged maps of Africa, the East Indies, and India. It is this map of India, made in 1561, which is at the centre of a controversy.

Two printed versions of the map are available. One is printed as 'the second of three maps' in the second edition of Ramusio's work, and the other is preserved in the British

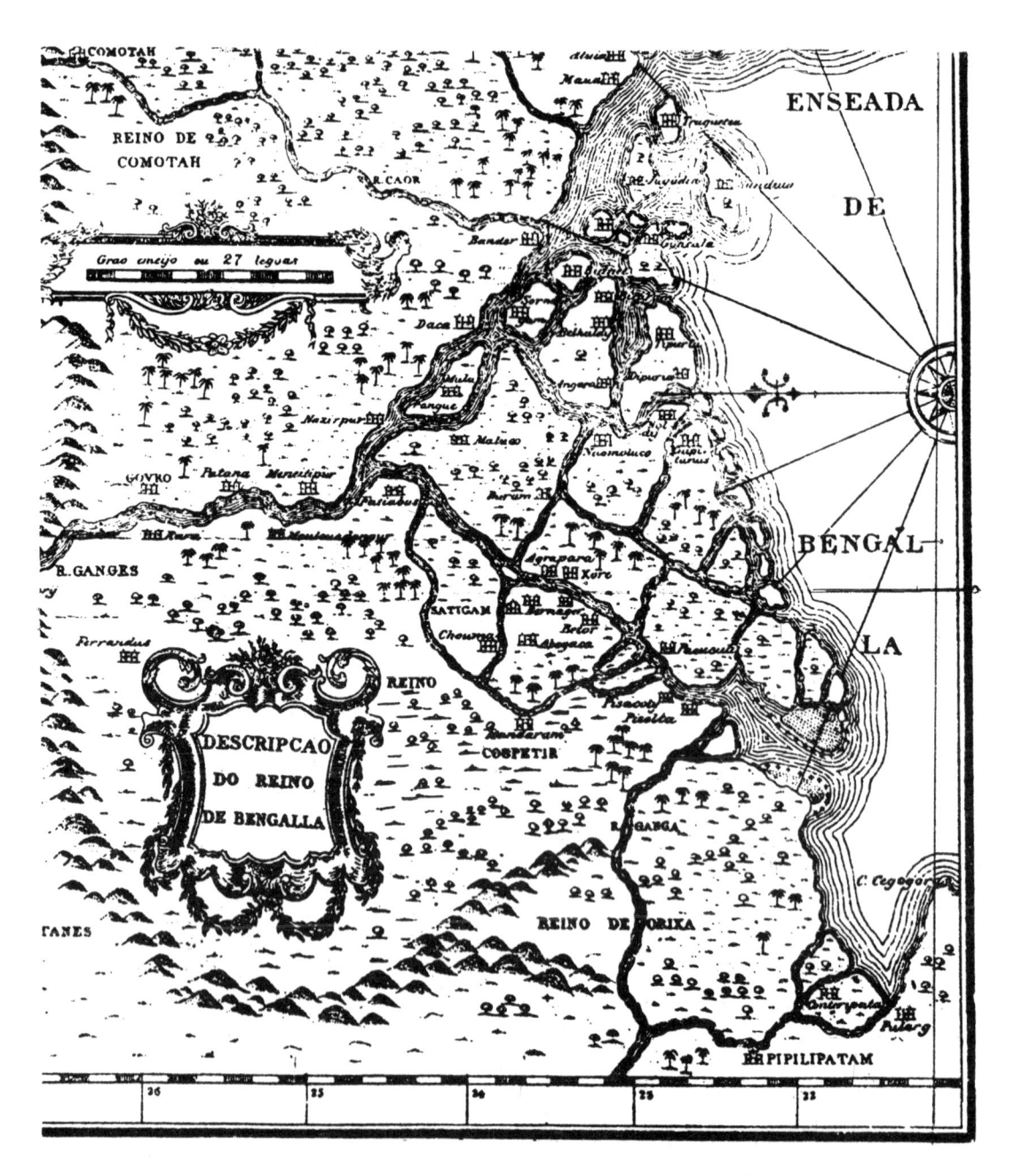

Map 3.1: Detail of Map of Bengal by Joao de Barros (*c.* 1550).

Museum, as map no. K 115(7). The first is reproduced on page 110 of *India Within the Ganges* by Susan Gole, and the other, a copy appearing as plate 2 in the *Historical Records of the Survey of India*, vol. I, by Col. R.H. Phillimore. We may not go into the controversy regarding the authorship of the maps, as it is not relevant to the subject of the present investigation, except that the second map, looking identical to the first one, bears the following words: 'Ferando Bertoli exc. 1565' written outside the left-hand bottom margin. The first one is ascribed to Gastaldi, a promising map-maker of the latter-half of the sixteenth century. Closer examination indicates that the two maps are not from the same wooden block, as there are many dissimilarities, including the two giant fish missing in the second map while the islands in the regions are retained. Apart from these variations, the geographical contents in both the maps look similar.

Both the maps are south oriented, showing Ptolemaic influence so far as the coastline of the subcontinent is concerned. On the landmass of India, since the northern plain is not shown, only the lower Bengal region of the Ganges is marked, with no delta formation. The Ganga of the peninsula is retained. The Western Ghats are also marked. The two tributaries, the Crusuar and the Benhar, issuing out of places about 2° of latitude south of the Tropic of Cancer, and joining together, the river Ganga flows northeast, then moves southeast to fall into 'olge de Bengala'. Though the 'Ganga' is drawn on the maps as per the description of Barros, the maps do not contain any place-name on the entire course of the river, except Romana and Satigan in the Orissa region where it falls into the Bay of Bengal. The main feature regarding 'Ganga' shown on these maps is that it flows its course remaining north of the Tropic. The region 'Dely' (Delhi) is marked below the line. The river Indus is shown coming north-southward, almost perpendicular, and falls into the Gulf of Cambey. Cochin is written near the tip of the peninsula, in the south, and the territory on its east is named Narsinga. On the whole, the entire map is a crude attempt, with entire regions between many rivers shown as mountainous, with no blank spaces and very few place-names. No longitudinal values are given to the map. Thus not much information regarding 'eastern' and 'western' boundaries, or we may say the rivers Ganges and the Indus, provided.

The next map of the century simply but beautifully illustrates parts of Indian geography. It was drawn by Father Monserrate,[7] a member of the first Jesuit mission to the Court of Akbar, the great Mughal Emperor. Monserrate landed at Goa, then travelled to Daman, Surat, and finally reached Fatehpur Sikri, the seat of the Emperor. It was in 1581 that he got the opportunity to accompany the Emperor on his march to Kabul. Being a trained surveyor, he measured the route whenever he could and took astronomical observations at as many places as he could. Though the map is partly based on measured routes and astronomically observed places, with latitudinal and longitudinal scales on the margins, it gives the route from Surat through Delhi to Kabul. But by placing Surat east of Goa in longitude, Monserrate made his map between Agra and Kabul about 4° too far to the east. His map gives the topography of the western Himalaya mountains, and upper courses of the rivers Jumna and Indus. It seems he had no knowledge of the region east of the Jumna because the river Ganges shown by him looks like a tributary of the Jumna. It is shown flowing almost in north-south direction on 124° longitude, probably counted from Pope meridian as revised by the Treaty of Torsedillas of 1494.[8]

Monserrate was perhaps the only map-maker of the sixteenth century who speculated on the source of the river Ganges in his map of 1590. When he saw the Himalaya for the first time from south of Ambala on his way to Kabul in 1581, he expressed his thoughts thus: 'Mount Imaus, which local people call Cumaun, burst into view, covered with snow, and throwing off a chilly wind. . . . The inhabitants say that the sources of the Jumna are in this region, where the mountains slope westward towards the plains of Delhi. The Ganges rises on a slope that faces east, with a difference in longitude of 280 miles, and on the same latitude, 30° and a third.'[9] He has also shown Lake Manasarovar in his map.

The next map of the century worth our examination is that by Giacopo di Gastaldi (also spelled as Jiacomo Gastaldi, Jacopo Gastaldi and Jacobo Gastaldi), a professional and innovative cartographer who became prominent in Venice, Italy, during the mid-sixteenth century. In 1548, Gastaldi issued an Italian edition of Ptolemy's *Geographia* which contained *Tabula Asiae X* (Map 3.2).[10] Being completely in Ptolemaic tradition, no fresh comments are needed.

As was the general practice with the geographers of the day, new maps, called 'modern' maps were added to this publication by Gastaldi. One of these was a map of south India, entitled *Calecut Nuova Tavola* (Map 3.3).[11]

This was a pre-1550 map and therefore, did not contain the southern 'Ganga'. Ramusio requested Gastaldi to prepare a map of Asia from his great atlas for his book.[12]

This book was printed in 1554. After the first edition was out, a fire broke out in 1557 in the printing press. The controversy regarding the map in Ramusio's second edition of *Delle Navigatione et Viaggi*, published in Venice in 1565 (Map 3.4), has been touched upon earlier.

Gastaldi's map of 1554 for Ramusio's book is also of southern India, but the coastal line intends right from the delta region of the Ganges in the east, around the peninsula, up to the southwest of Arabia, close to Eden. The map also shows a portion of the Persian Gulf. The map is south oriented and is drawn in very bold form, giving out very little information. It looks almost amateurish, unlike Gastaldi's other maps. It retains the peninsular 'Ganga' but does not cover the area of the Marco Polo's lake 'Chiamay' in the northeast of Assam. The 'Ganga' is shown coming out of the mountains, below the Tropic, moving northeastward in a parabolic form, crossing the Tropic and for a major part of its course, remains north of the Tropic, before falling into the Bay of Bengal just below the Tropic, near the seashore. 'Dely', the capital of the kingdom of the same name, is marked below the Tropic, on the banks of the 'Ganga'. Narsinga is shown east of Cochin in the extreme south of the peninsula.

In 1561, Gastaldi re-engraved a part-map of his Asia of the same year, showing India separately.[13] This shows the importance being attached to India by the geographers and cartographers of the day alike. This map too includes de Barros' information. The mythical river 'Ganga' with its tributaries is prominently shown with 'Delli' on its banks. Interestingly, the entire course of the river remains below the Tropic of Cancer and the river flows almost in a straight line in the northeast-east direction to the Bay of Bengal. Marco Polo's lake 'Chiamay', Pinto's lake 'Singapamor' (1614), is also marked between the parallels of the Tropic and 27° in the present northeast region of Myanmar (Burma).

The above discussed four sets maps of Gastaldi: (i) Ptolemy's *Geographia,* in the Italian

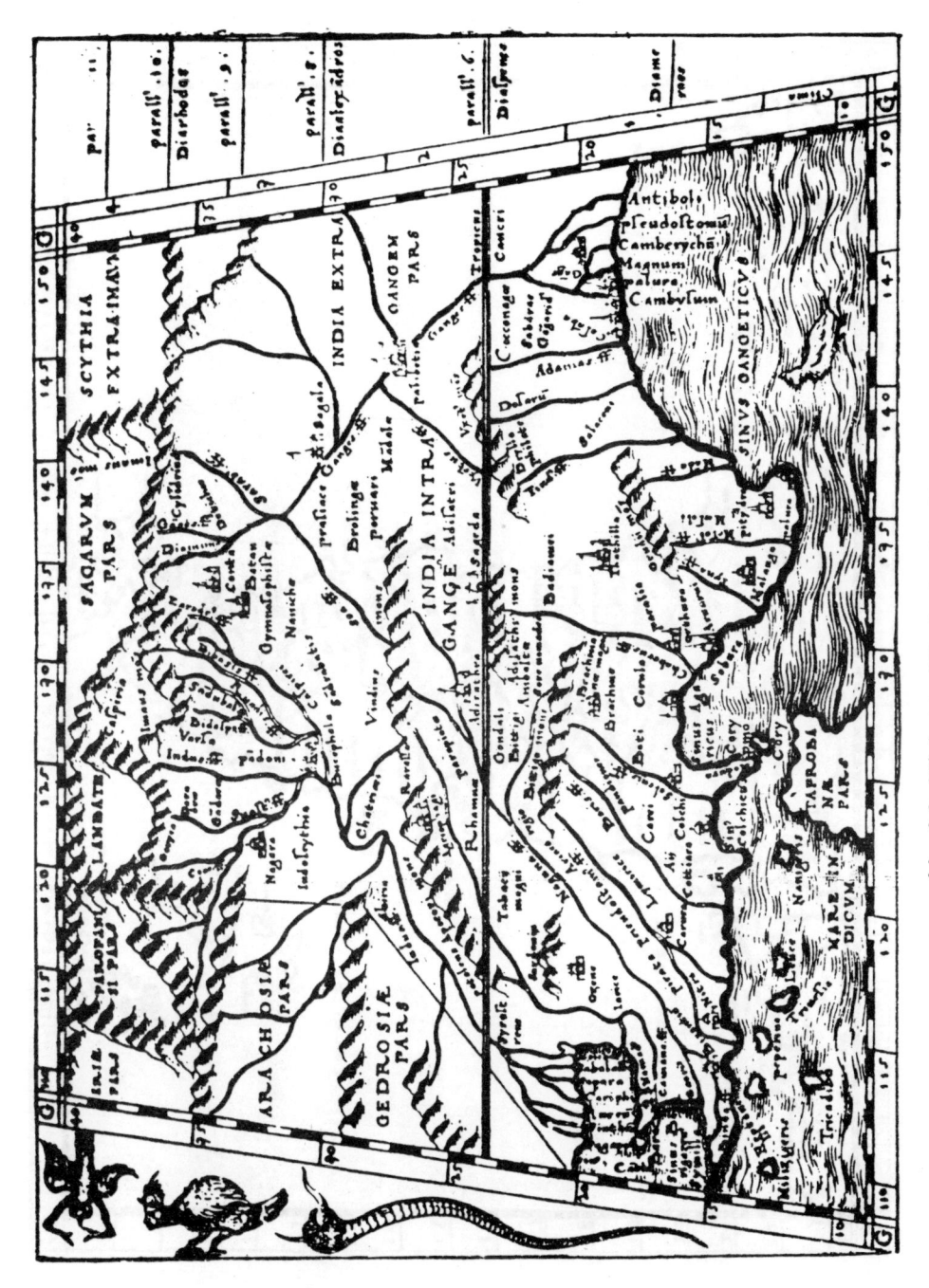

Map 3.2: *Tabula Asiae X* by Jacobo Gastaldi (1548).

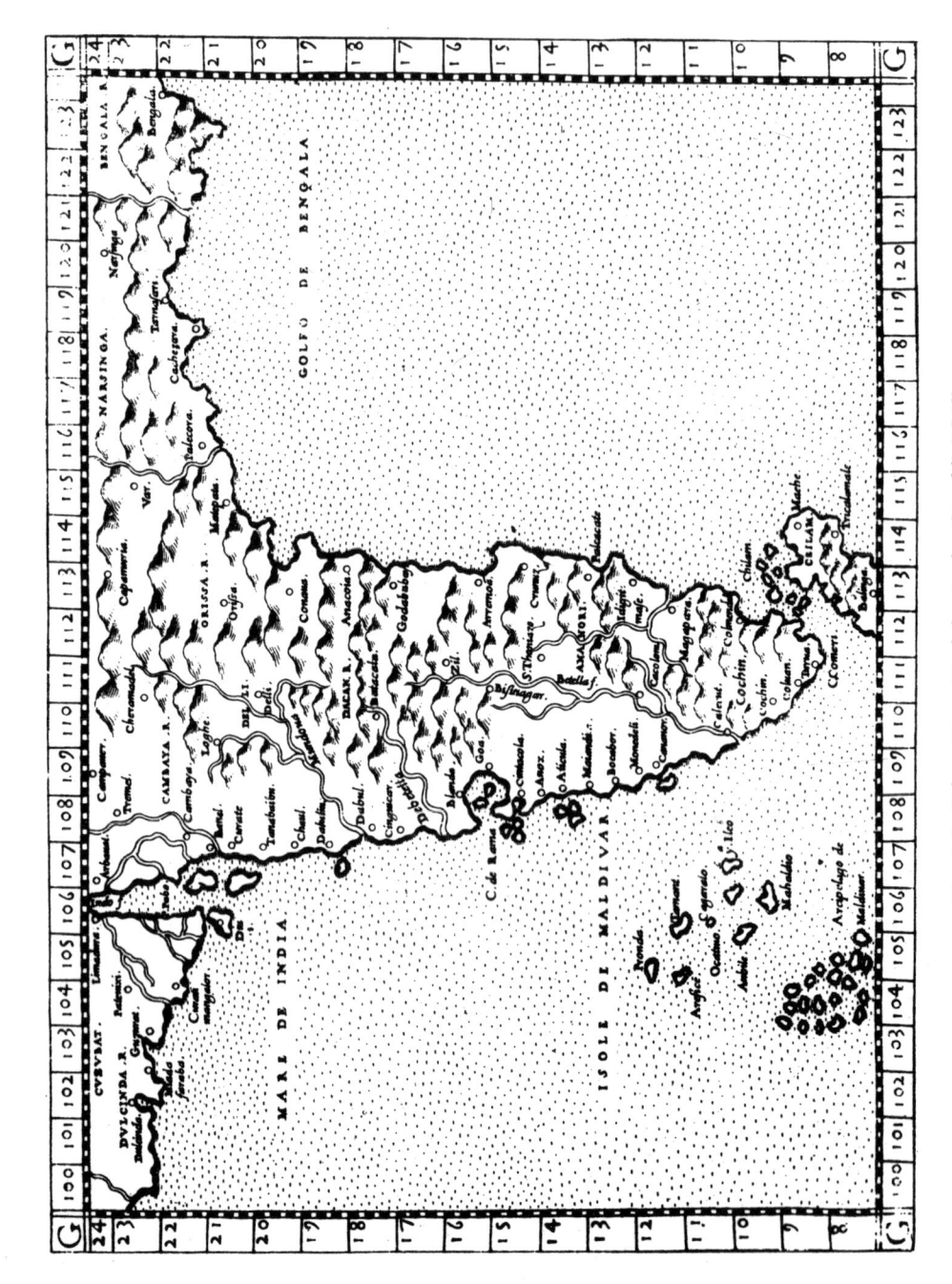

Map 3.3: *Calecut Nuova Tavola* by Jacobo Gastaldi (1548).

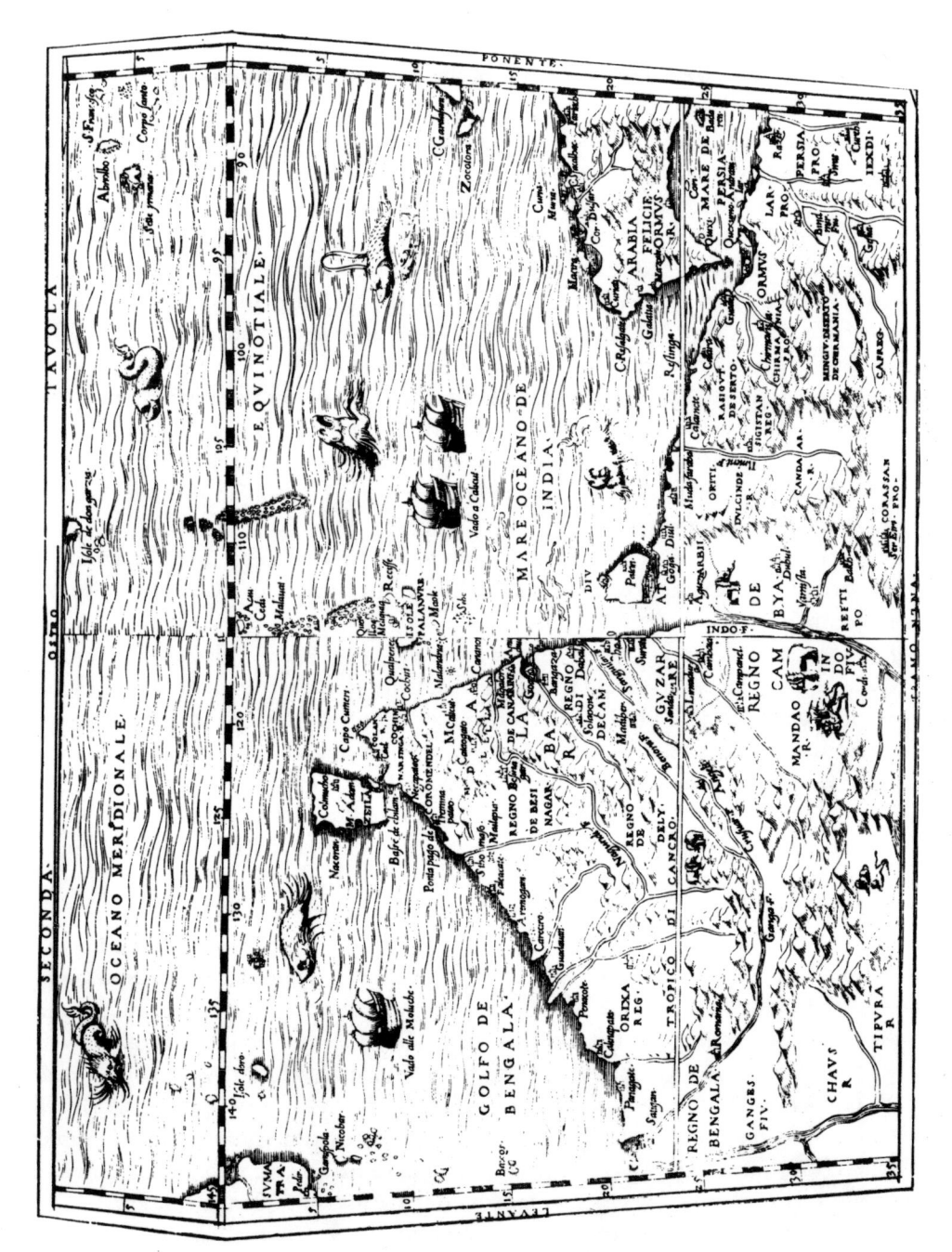

Map 3.4: *Second Tavola* by Jacobo Gastaldi (1565).

version, published in 1548; (ii) 'modern' map of south India (1548) attached with the Ptolemy's atlas; (iii) Gastaldi's map of India (1554) for Ramusio's book; and (iv) his own map of a part of Asia (1561), showing India could well be taken as nearly perfect examples of the types of maps of India that were seen during the rest of the sixteenth and coming seventeenth and most of the eighteenth centuries.

These illustrate well, the confusion in the minds of the then cartographers and map-makers so far as the geography of the Indian subcontinent is concerned. The so-called 'travel' accounts or narratives would carry, as we shall see, major fallacies and controversies, without exception, whatever might be the status, reputation, and credibility of the cartographer, even when empirical information, contrary to the above notions was available.

Moving further down the list of geographical writers and map-makers of the sixteenth century, Fernao Lopes de Castanheda (1500-59) was a well-read man with a scholarly temperament. He began his literary career after spending about a decade in the East, especially in peninsular India since 1528. Back home, he interviewed persons who had been to India before publishing his first book *Historia do descobrimento e conquista da India pelos Portuguezes*, in 1551.[14] In all, he has ten books to his credit, seven in his lifetime and three posthumously. His works are full of first-hand empirical geographical information about India useful to geographers and map-makers.

There were many others whose contribution to world-geography and the science of cartography cannot be brushed aside, however, their contribution to the Indian scenario is far less in comparison.

Gerard Mercator (1512-94) the Latinized name of Gerard Kremer, possessed an unusual combination of theoretical and practical knowledge. A. Flander, was a land surveyor, engraver, maker of mathematical and astronomical instruments, and cartographer. He had been a student of cosmography at the university of Louvain and had acquired cartographic techniques also. During his lifetime he was recognized as a skilled and innovative cartographer. Even now, he is remembered as the inventor of the 'Mercator Projection' maps, which are still being used extensively. But his contribution to our theme of investigation is almost negligible.

Next, in chronological order, comes the famous world atlas of Dutchman, Abraham Ortels, better known by his Latinized name of Ortelius of Antwerp.[15] His atlas, which had in a way replaced the famous atlas of Ptolemy, was called *Theatrum Orbis Terrarum*. This was originally issued independently by Ortelius in 1567 as *Asia orbis partium maximae nova descripto*.[16] On this map, he showed a large lake 'Singapamor', which later map-makers called 'Chiamay Lake', the first major fallacy on the maps of India. But Ortelius' map did not show the Himalaya. The river Ganges was shown flowing in north-south direction, with no mountains to impede or change its course. On the other hand, about half a century later, in 1619, Baffin did not show this in his empirical map drawn as per the information gathered in an interview with Thomas Roe. Subsequently, within ten years, this lake made a reappearance in almost all the maps of the known map-makers, and remained there for more than a century.

In 1598, another useful and practical book came out. Jan Huyghen van Linschoten (1563-1611) was an ambitious man who came to India and stayed in Goa from 1583 to 1589 as a dependent of the archbishop of Goa. While there, he collected material for his *Itinerario*, which came out in 1594. The book became popular and was translated into several languages. It gave direct impetus for the formation of the Dutch and British East India Companies' in the early seventeenth century. This even 'served to maintain public interest in attempts to break into the Portuguese monopoly of direct oriental trade by sea'. It contained some of the best maps of the sixteenth century.

Linschoten's[17] map of 1596 (Map 3.5) does not have coordinates but a beautiful compass-rose with rhumb lines all over are there. The territories containing the sources of the Indus and the Ganges are blocked with panels giving some detail of the map and the scale adopted. The southern Ganga is marked, but is named river Guenga, and its two tributaries in the upper region, Crusuar and Benora are seen rising from the eastern phase of the Western Ghats, a single mountain range going north-south, and dividing the peninsula into two almost equal east-west parts. As in other maps, the Ganga does not cross the Tropic of Cancer but remains south of it throughout its course. Delli kingdom is marked in the region between the two upper tributaries of the Guenga, while the town is shown at the junction of another unnamed tributary.

The legends of mystery and sanctity attached to the Ganges and its source since the early historical period or even earlier forced successive writers to comment upon it. Seventeenth century was no exception. Historian Terry wrote extensively about the source of the Ganges in 1655 after his journey to the source in 1612.[18] The renowned cartographer D'Anville used the details given by Terry in his map, and extensively quoted him in his writings.

The legend that the Ganges springs out of a large rock cut in the shape of a cow's head near Hardwar, and is being worshipped and venerated by almost everyone in India, attracted the attention of the Mughal Emperor Akbar.[19] Intrigued, he sent a fact-finding team to Gangotri, the supposed place of the origin of the Ganges, towards the end of the sixteenth century.

Around the same time, Ptolemy's influence nearly disappeared from the cartographic scenario, and Ptolemy and his maps became for many cartographers of the day, a thing of the past, 'a revered antiquarian curiosity'.[20]

Delving into the details of the seventeenth-century mapping activities of some known map-makers when fallacies about Indian are perpetuated and carried on unchecked centuries, for together with relevant narratives of first-hand accounts of famous travellers of the time, may give us answers: to some perplexing questions.

Leaving aside the maps with Ptolemic ideas, the seventeenth-century maps are supposed to have been drawn with more empirical data. These maps have an interesting, long, and chequered history. These may reveal the lure of the 'Ganga' of the later map-makers which remained as unresistable and controversial as the other fallacies discussed. These would also illustrate the gradual changes that came about in the perception of India and its dimensions in the minds of cartographers and people at large in the West.

During this century, the Indian Ocean was a scene of great maritime activity. There were many individual European travellers as well as officially sponsored companies of traders whose vessels moved to and from Europe to India and beyond. It was the time when traders and travellers did not openly dare to venture into the interiors of India. They mostly remained

Map 3.5: Detail of *Orientalis* by Jan Huygen van Linschoten (1596).

in seashore towns. Their 'travel accounts', with spicy stories, when published, generated great interest among the general public in Europe. It resulted in tremendous demand for such books and the latest maps of the regions showing details of the discoveries of strange lands and their peoples. Some book publishers were excellent map-makers as well.

Following the setting up of the East India Company in 1600, the English too began to participate in the maritime trade activities in eastern waters. They sailed on their first voyage in 1608. William Hawkins, the captain of the ship, visited Surat. He also met Mughal Emperor, Jahangir at Ajmer. In 1612, after establishing a small settlement in Surat, he left for England. Not long after, the English were able to establish settlements at Ahmedabad, Burhanpur, and even in the heart of the Mughal empire, at Ajmer and Agra. The English factory, as the settlement was called in those days, at Surat henceforth became the chief English settlement in the East.

In 1615, on the request of the Company Sir Thomas Roe, was sent by King James of England as ambassador to the court of the Mughal Emperor. Later, Sir Thomas Roe accompanied the Mughal Emperor on one of his military expeditions to the northwest of India. Roe finally left for England in 1619 on board the ship, *Anne*. Coincidentally, the first mate of the ship, William Baffin, was very much interested in map-making. With the intention of making a map of India at some future date, he tried to extract as much geographical and cartographic information from Roe as Roe, too, was interested in and excited to describe in detail his observations of the country which he had an opportunity to travel and see for himself, that too under the direct patronage of the highest personality of the land, the Mughal Emperor, and talking to his ministers and courtiers as well as to the general public. Armed with authentic first-hand information from such an authority, which lent a great deal of credibility, Baffin was excited about his future project. In 1619, he published his map of India (Map 3.6),[21] which became popular overnight.

Being such an important and one of the earliest of the seventeenth-century maps, it deserves a close look. How far did it serve to sharpen the image of India in the Europeans?

It seems Baffin was unaware of the dominant historical and political currents of events, and so also of broad geographical and political divisions in the Indian subcontinent. Or, was it because, Roe sitting in the Mughal court, could not precisely describe the general layout of the provinces, especially that of Orissa. Mere statement that it was at the 'utmost east of the Mogul's territories beyond the Bay of Bengal',[22] perhaps confused Baffin. The kingdom of Orissa, therefore, is seen at two places in his map, with its important town of Jagernat (Jagannath) placed between Bengal and Myanmar (Burma) the other Orissa, written as Orixa, is at its proper place, meaning thereby that Baffin was not aware that both the provinces, Orixa and Odessa, were two names for the same territory. Again, Patna is not correctly placed on the river Ganges; it is shown on the river Son, a tributary of the Ganges; Lahore is marked on the Indus, and so on. The historian Orme's remark that the Baffin's map is 'curious for knowledge misplaced',[23] is quite appropriate. About the Ganges, supposed eastern boundary of India for the early European map-makers till then, Baffin has shown the Ganges, but his Jumna rises about 20 miles west of Delhi. The Ganges flows down the mount Caucasus, through a 'cow's mouth at Hardwar, then flows in the south-southeast direction and meets

Map. 3.6: A Description of the East India Company in *The Empire of the Great Mogul* by William Baffin (1619).

the sea. The 'cow's mouth', obviously, could not have been a living cow, but a rocky area, somewhat resembling a cow's head. This was later distorted by the map-makers, who began showing a small lake instead. The map, however, does not cover the mythical 'Chiamay Lake' area in Assam.

Baffin, like all others of the period, shows the river Guenga (Ganga) in peninsular India. Had this been described to Baffin by Roe himself, or was Baffin himself aware of it, or he just 'followed the crowd'? The answer is not easy to get. But like the others, he has included the peninsular Guenga (Ganga), and thus contributed to the perpetuation of the existence of the mythical river. However, his Guenga springs out in Orixa (Orissa), with the two supporting tributaries Grusuar and Benhora, and flows northeast-eastward, and meets the 'Gulfo de Bengala', much below the Ganges.

Despite its drawbacks, most of the prominent map-makers of the seventeenth century depended heavily on this map and copied it unhesitatingly and almost consistently.

Quarter of a century later, in 1637, a Dutch cartographer brought out peculiar map of Asia wherein two rivers—both, perhaps, interpretations of the same river with two different sources—were shown on one map, with similar sounding names given to them. This map was the creation of Rumold,[24] grandson of the renowned cartographer, Gerard Mercator. The holy river of India, the Ganges, once thought by the Westerners as the eastern boundary of India, is shown in Rumold's map as flowing from the Central Asian plateau almost due east, and falling into the China Sea.[25] The other river, named Guenga (Ganga of other map-makers), is depicted in peninsular India, and merges into the Bay of Bengal flowing from the north. Interestingly, Palimbotra (Patliputra or modern Patna) is marked on the former river, near the place where the river meets the China Sea, while Delli (Delhi) is shown near the upper course of the latter river. Such cartographic absurdities could, perhaps, be the result of map-makers' beliefs in the abundant geographical and literary fantasies and myths about India, the Indian peoples, their lives, and rituals being circulated in the West since very early in the BC era. This has already been touched upon earlier. But, Rumold must have been aware of the scholarship and methodology of his grandfather Gerard Mercator, the famous map-maker whose name is still remembered with reverence. He would surely have gone through the geographical literature accumulated and available to him around the period but, it seems, he preferred to depend upon the wrong ones, and hence the publishing of such a fantastic map of Asia. But one thing is clear—the Ganges is no longer treated as the 'eastern boundary of India', and there is earth and life in the region beyond the Ganges, eastward.

Seventeenth century saw a different scenario in the cartographic world. Almost all the maritime nations of the West competing in the Indian Ocean had, during this century, got some foothold on the Indian mainland. Some were moving into the interior of the country in almost every direction. Foreigners going to the interior by boats on the river Ganges in the north was a common sight. Some had penetrated even to the region of its source. A number of maps had, therefore, come up in Europe based on geographical data collected by visitors during the seventeenth century.

Baffin's map was the model for most map-makers till the end of the century. There were some who announced that their maps were 'revised', and 'new', but nothing new was added to the geography of India. The map-makers were in an embarrassing situation as very few travellers to India were able to give exact astronomical locations of the places they travelled through.

One of the earliest travel literature of this century that became very popular came out in 1614. This was Mendes Pinto's account of his journey to the supposed place of origin of the holy river Ganges. A Portuguese sailor, his account, along with other narratives of his wanderings in China and the South-East Asia, mentions a large lake somewhere in the present south-east of Tibet, or in the north-east of Assam. He called it as lake Singapamor,[26] thus corroborating Marco Polo's version of such a lake (Chiamay) in the region in the thirteenth century.

Another well-known traveller was Jean Baptiste Tavernier who made several journeys through India between 1640-67.[27] This French diamond merchant-traveller confirmed the existence of the lake. He also kept record of the distance travelled stage by stage.[28] Describing the lake, he says that several rivers flow from it, and it is situated in the 29th and 30th degree latitudes. This created confusion amongst the then mapmakers, but almost all the later cartographers accepted the lake's existence for more than a century.

Some seventeenth-century cartographers who contributed to Indian geography were: Jaos de Barros (or Jean de Barros)[29] (Map 3.1), the great chronicler and map-maker Gerard Mercator and his grandson,[30] Rumold (1512-94), Hondius family[31] (1563-1651), traditional rivals in map-making to the contemporary Bleau family[32] (1571-1673); Vischar family[33] (1587-1702); Jan Jansson[34] (1596-1644), brother-in-law of Henricum Hondius; Frederick de Wit[35] (1630-1706); Dankert family[36] (c. 1633-1727), and Vincenzo Maria Coronelli[37] (1650-1718) (Maps 3.11.1-3.11.3); Nicolas Sanson[38] (1600-67) (Maps 3.7, 3.8) and his family (1600-1708), fore-runners of the great French school of cartography; Robert Morden[39] (d. 1705) (Map 3.9), the English map-maker. All these and others mentioned earlier were very active during the period. Not all the maps of these map-makers are available for inspection, but those that are accessible indicate that all fell prey to the temptations of giving the 'latest accurate maps' to the readers and continued publishing the fantasies and fallacies, in one respect or the other, exhibiting thereby a state of confusion so far as the Indian segment is concerned.

In the middle of the seventeenth century, Nicolas Sanson D'Abbeville[40] brought two maps of India (Maps 3.7, 3.8) which were translated into English by Richard Blome for his book in 1670. Nicolas Sansson was the 'Geographer to the King of France, and was generally considered as the pioneer of geography in France'.[41] His maps title nothing more and follow Baffin to a large extent. Pieter van der Aa[42] (1659-1733), a Hollander (Map 3.10)—published large number of maps for various writers, but the geography of India on all these maps remained where it was when Baffin's map first came out in 1619 (Map 3.6).

However, some map-makers of the seventeenth century showed some awareness about these fallacies, as is apparent from their published maps. But, unfortunately, they 'followed the crowd'. Vincenzo Maria Coronelli,[43] an innovative cartographer of Italy who kept into the country's tradition of excellence in map-making even as Italy declined as a maritime power, was one such map-maker. He was a Franciscan friar and the Cosmographer to the

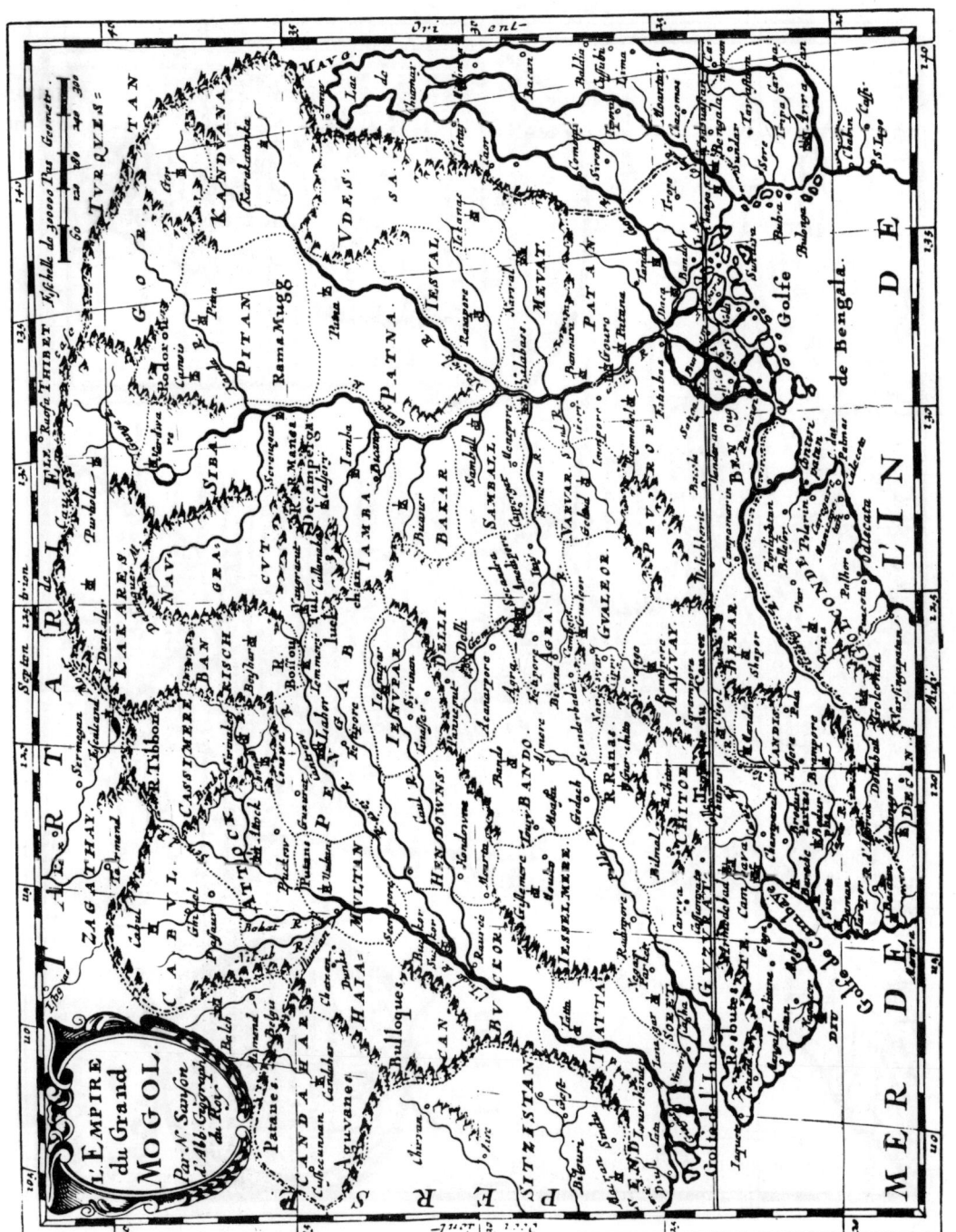

Map. 3.7: *L'Empire du Grand Mogul* by Nocolas Sanson Abville (1652).

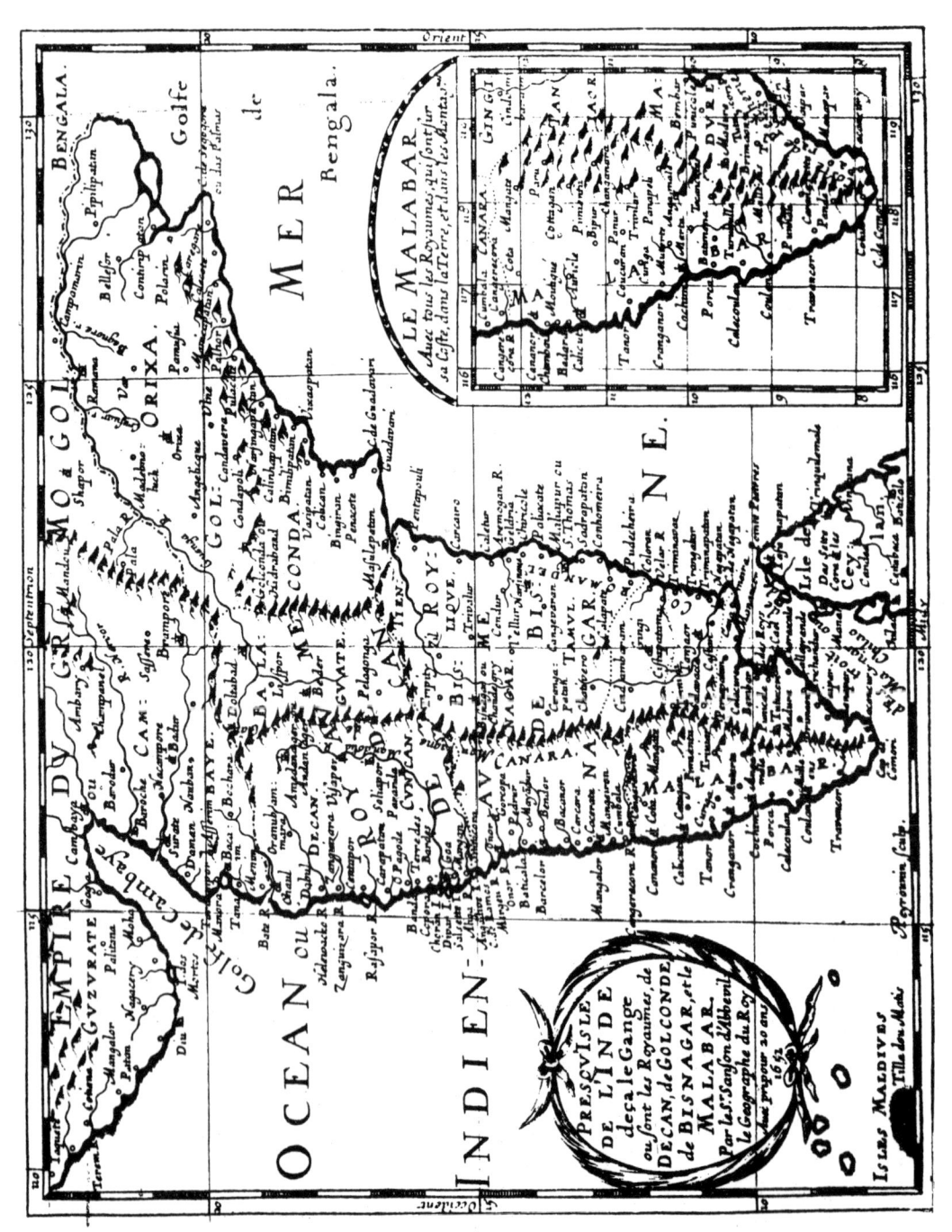

Map 3.8: *Presqu' Inde de L'Inde* by Nicolas Sanson Abville (1652).

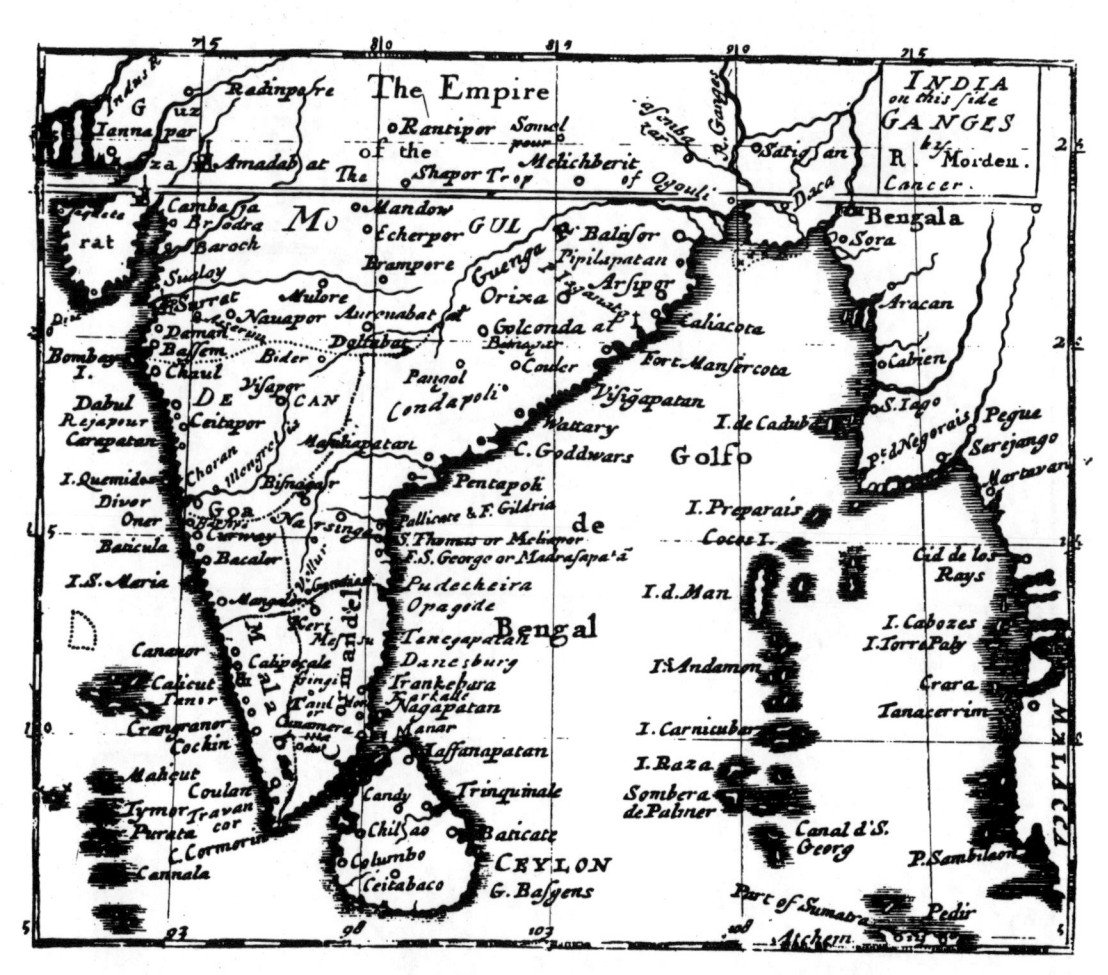

Map. 3.9: *The Peninsula on this side Ganges* by Robert Morden (1680).

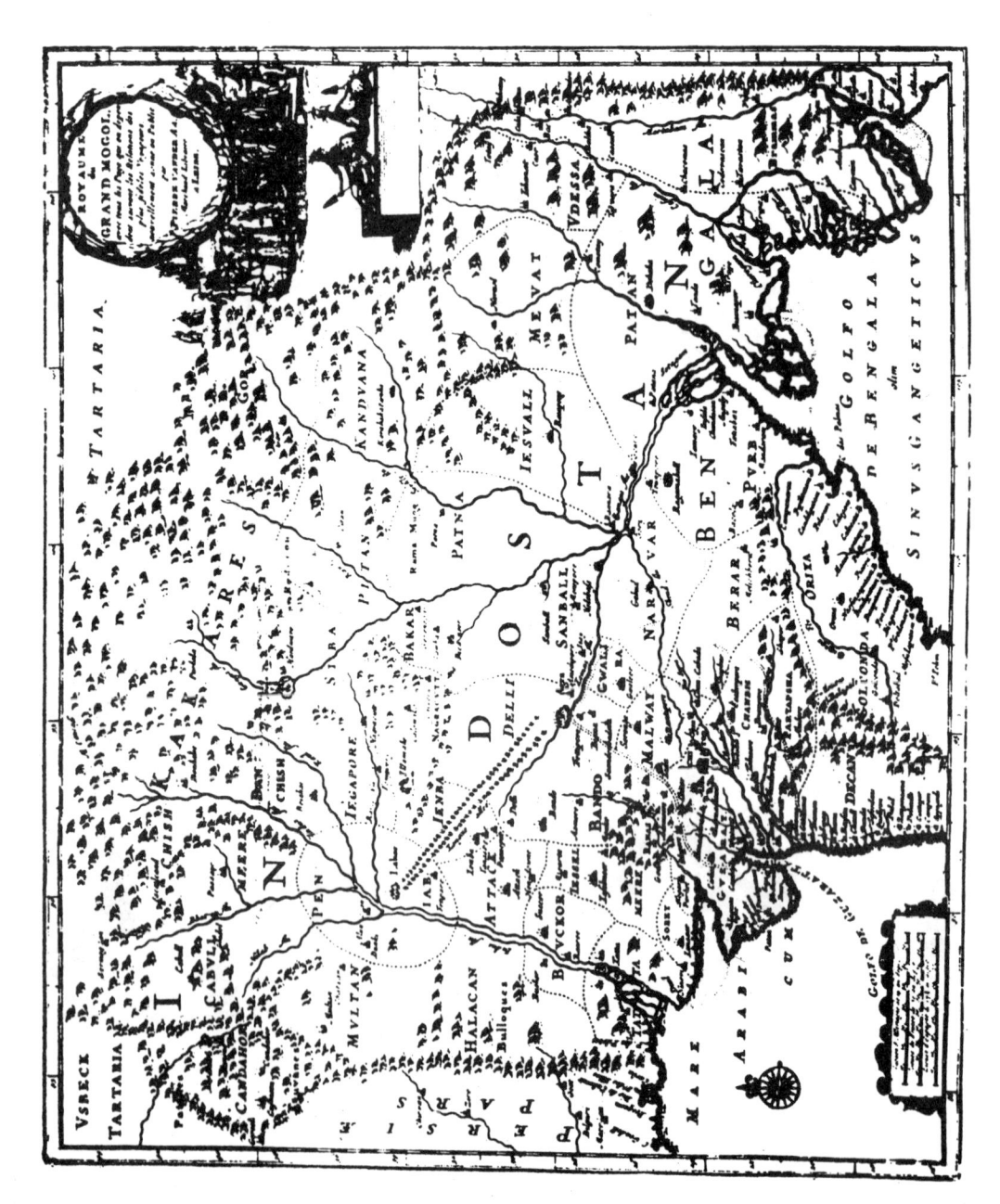

Map 3.10: *Royaume de Grand Mogol* by Pieter van der Aa (1729).

Republic of Venice. In 1680, he founded the world's first geographical society, *Academia Cosmografica degli Argonauti*.[44] His two maps, *Impero del Gram Mogol*[45] (Maps 3.11.1-3.11.3) and *Peninsola dell' Indo*,[46] were well received by the map-makers.

Like other maps of the period, Coronelli's maps contained the usual fallacies perpetuated by other map-makers. His maps, however, differ in as much as they are bereft of much geographical details about the Indian mainland. The drafting of the topographical features is quite bold. His information about the sources of the Indus and the Ganges (Map 3.11.1) and the details of their upper courses seems scanty. The space is mostly filled with written notes on various rivers and place-names. As usual, the southern Ganga (Map 3.11.3) is present, quite bold in outline. Despite his reputation as a map-maker, Coronellis geography of the Indian mainland lacks serious application, unlike his information about lake 'Chiamay' (Map 3.11.2). This is evident from the notes written on the map regarding the flooding of the lake during certain months and so on.

As more and more map-makers began showing details of the interiors of Asia, including that of India during the seventeenth century, greater confusion prevailed amongst the map-makers about the origin and the course of the much revered Ganges. Some of the famous Dutch cartographers like Ortelius, Mercator, de Jode, and even Hondius and Bleau families, in their editions had shown the Chiamay Lake, originally described by Marco Polo in the thirteenth century, but not all of them, unlike Pinto, believed that the Ganges sprang from this lake. Dutch cartographers, unlike Baffin who pushed the Himalaya too far towards the north, omitted it, and were of the opinion that the Ganges issued out of a place far north in Central Asia, flowed down in the southward direction, with no Himalaya mountains between the source and the Sea of Bengala to obstruct or change its course.[47]

In the previous century, the credibility and fame of Barros and Ramusio probably caused the perpetuation, as we nave seen, of the fallacies about the geography of India. Mendes Pinto, as referred to earlier, inadvertently enhanced the confusion amongst the map-makers of the seventeenth century, especially those interested in the geography of India, by corroborating the existence of a large lake Singapamor in the far northeast of India, beyond the Ganges.[48] Pinto has stated in his book that four rivers flowed out of Singapamor, one going east, the second southeast, the third south, and the fourth was possibly the Ganges, flowing into the sea after passing through Bengala. Hondius, Bleau, and other later map-makers, however, refer to it as the Caor River.

On the other hand, historian Edward Terry in his *A Voyage to the East Indies* (1655), came up with the idea that the Ganges rose in the province of Siba. After emerging from the large rocks, arranged or cut by nature in the shape of a 'cow's head', the water of the Ganges formed itself into a full current and flowed down the plains of India.[49]

This was the cartographic scenario at the beginning of the eighteenth century with reference to India, the country which had become by this time, a major attraction for Western tourists, traders, politically inclined adventurers, religious zealots, and soldier-adventurists.

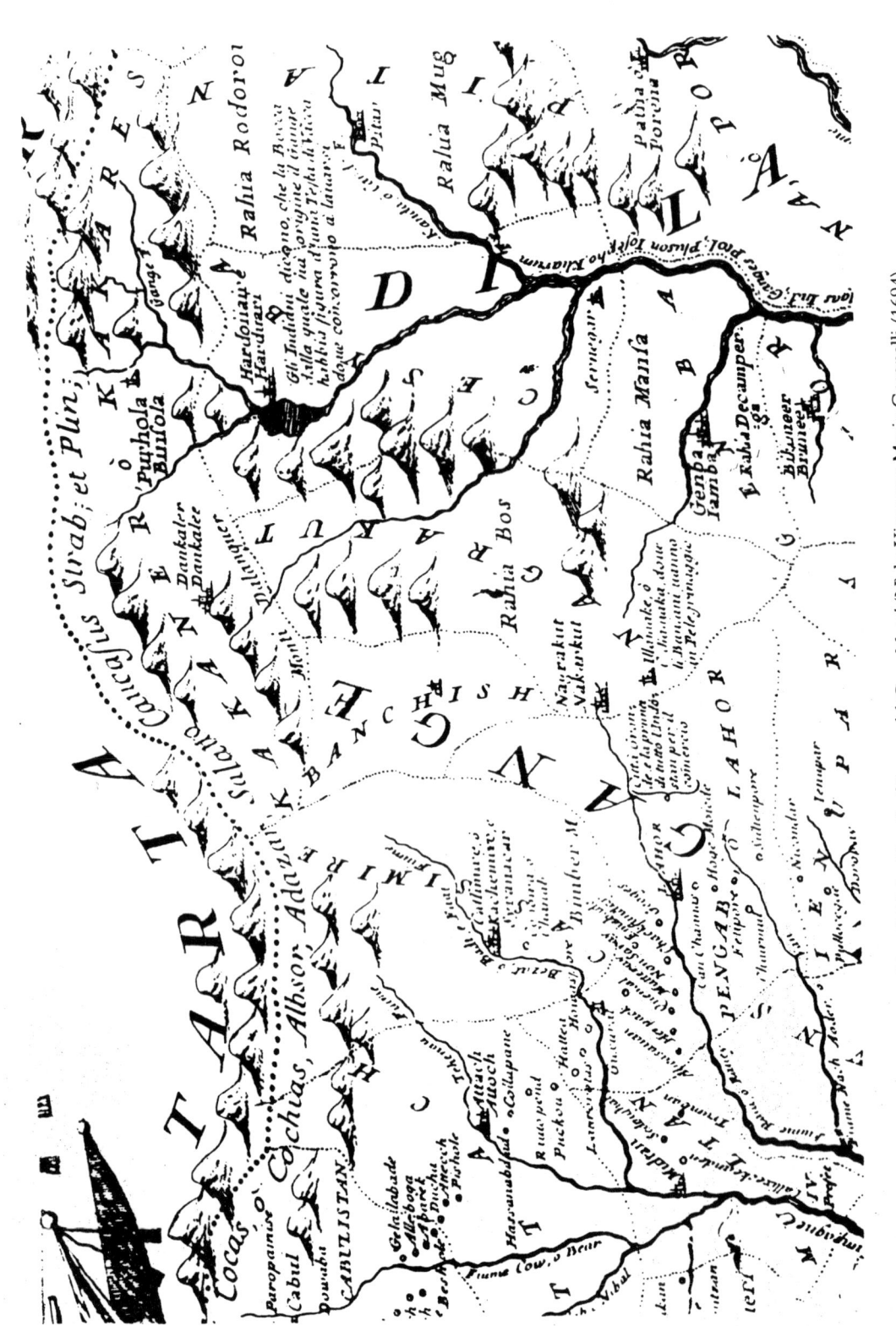

Map. 3.11.1: Detail of Impero del Gran Mogol (N) by Vincenzo Maria Coronelli (1694).

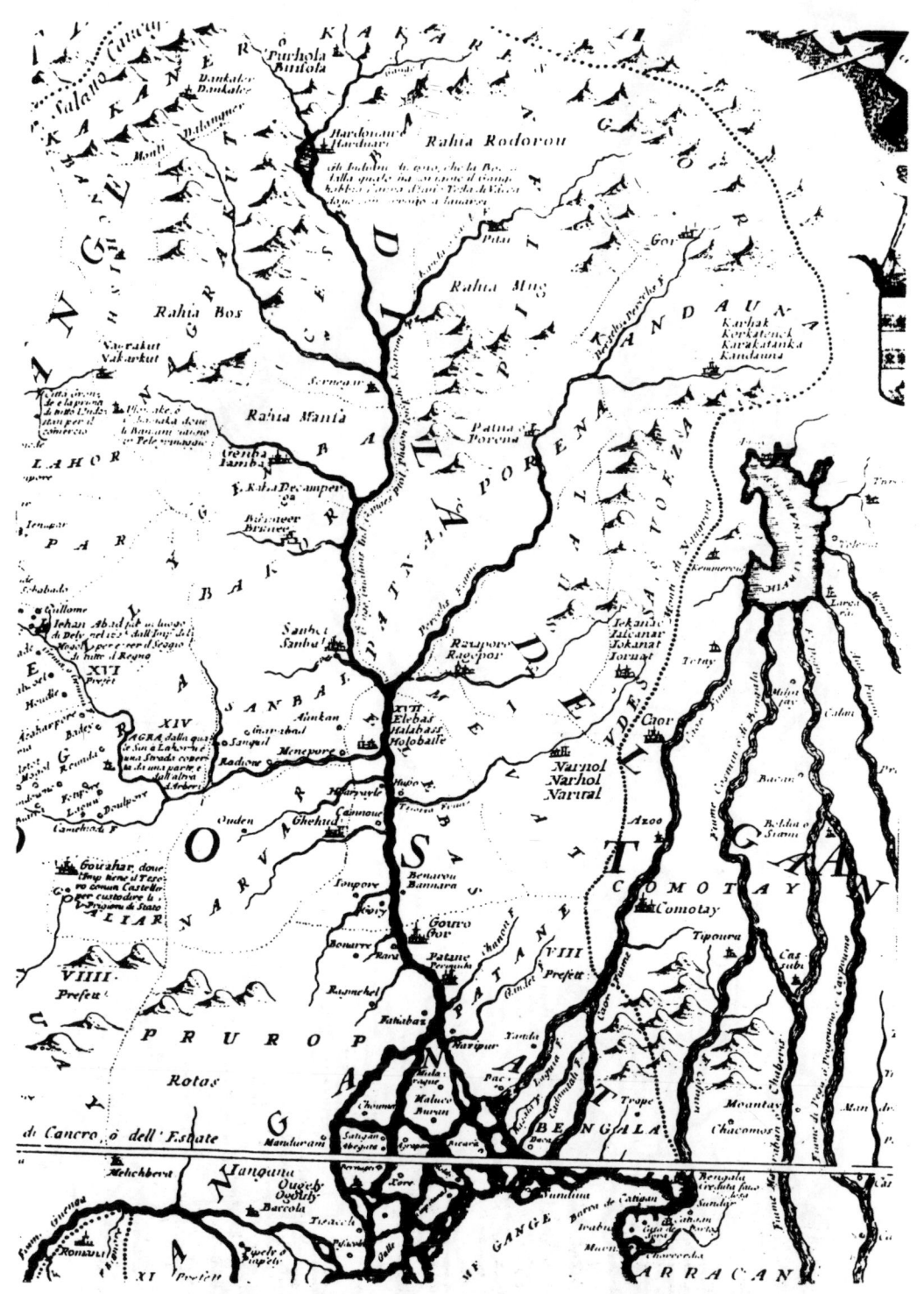

Map. 3.11.2: Detail of *Impero del Gran Mogol* (E) by Vincenzo Maria Coronelli (1694).

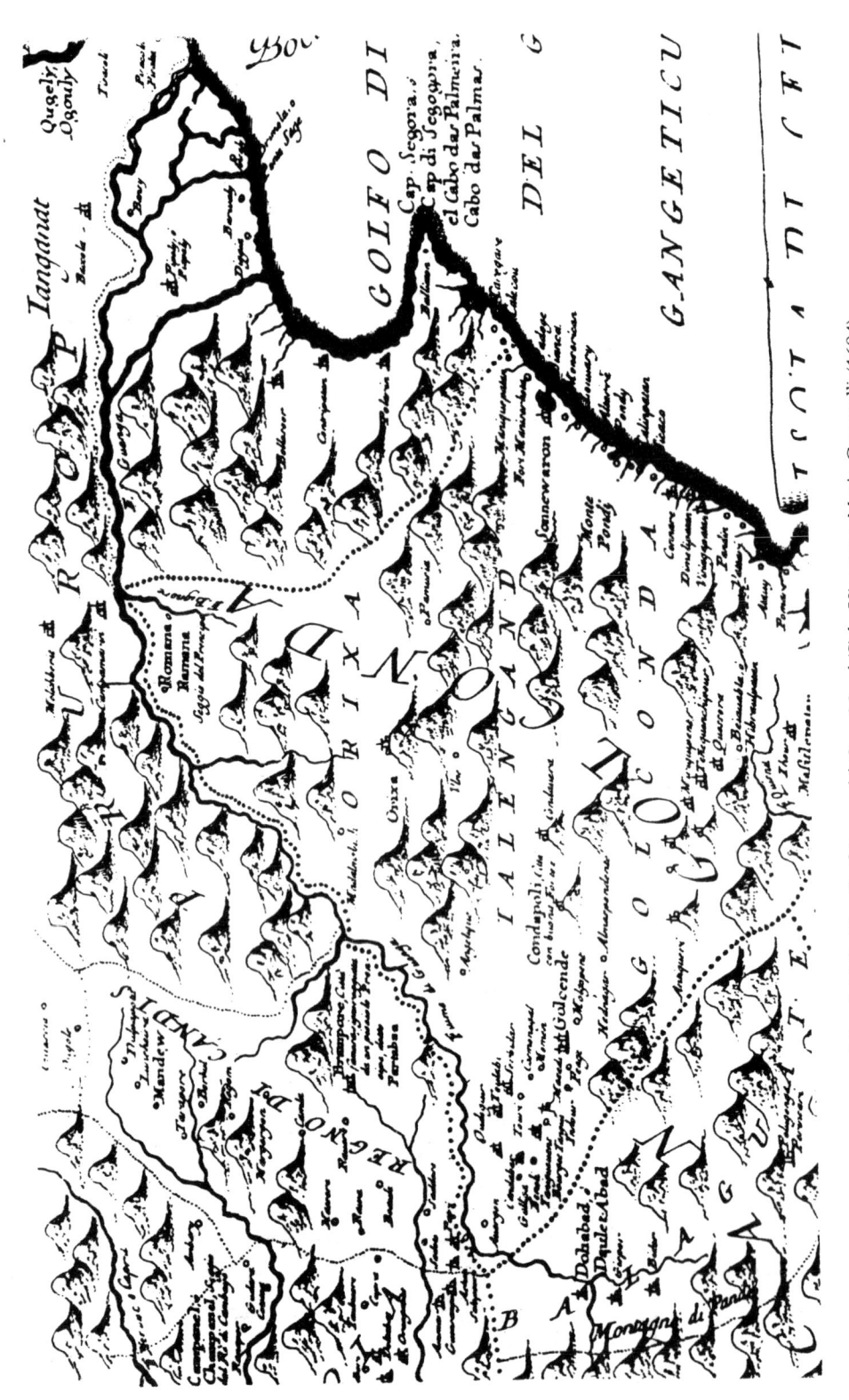

Map 3.11.3: Detail of *Impero del Gran Mogol* (S) by Vincenzo Maria Coronelli (1694).

NOTES

1. Donald F. Lach, *Asia in the Making of Europe*, 3 vols., Chicago and London, 1965-93, p. 185.
2. Ibid., p. 191.
3. Ibid.
4. William Herbert, *A Geographical Illustration of the Map of India*, 1759, p. 39.
5. *Asiatic Researches*, vol. xiv, 1822, pp. 436-7; R.H. Phillimore, *Historical Records of the Survey of India*, 5 vols., Dehra Dun, vol. 1, 1945, p. 78.
6. Donald F. Lach, op. cit., pp. 205-6.
7. Govt. of India, Original Records of Home Dept., Public Consultation A, dt. 29 Nov. 1784.
8. R.H. Phillimore, op. cit., vol. I, p. 10n; *Asiatic Researches*, vol. VIII, pp. 322-3.
9. Ibid., p. 68.
10. Susan Gole, *A Series of Early Printed Maps of India in Facsimile*, New Delhi, T. 7.
11. Ibid., T-M. 8.
12. Ibid., T-M. 9.
13. Ibid., *India Within the Ganges*, New Delhi, 1983, p. 110.
14. Donald F. Lach, op. cit., p. 187.
15. Lou Sebock (ed.), 'Introduction', in *Atlases Published in the Netherlands in the Rare Atlas Collection*, Ottawa: Publick Archives of Canada, National Map Collection, Provisional Series No. 1, 1793, p. x.
16. J.H. Parry, *The Age of Reconnaissance*, London, 1963, p. 113.
17. Susan Gole, *A Series*, op. cit., T-M. 10.
18. R.H. Phillimore, op. cit., vol. I, p. 71.
19. Ibid., vol. I, p. 71.
20. J.H. Parry, op. cit., p. 110.
21. Susan Gole, *A Series*, op. cit., M. 12.
22. Susan Gole, *Early Maps of India*, New Delhi, 1976, p. 49.
23. R.H. Phillimore, op. cit., vol. I, p. 209, quoted from Orme Manuscripts, 10, 134(169).
24. Susan Gole, *India Within*, op. cit., p. 60.
25. Ibid., p. 60.
26. Ibid.
27. R.H. Phillimore, op. cit., vol. I, p. 10.
28. Ibid., vol. I, p. 10.
29. Ibid., vol. I, p. 210, n. 6.
30. Susan Gole, *A Series*, op. cit., T-M. 4; Lou Sebock (ed.), *Netherlands Atlases*, op. cit., Introduction, pp. x-xi.
31. Ibid., T-M. 13; Ibid., Introduction, p. xi.
32. Ibid., T-M. 14; Ibid., Introduction, p. xi.
33. Lou Sebock (ed.), *Netherlands Atlases*, op. cit., Introduction, p. xii.
34. Ibid., T-M. 16; Introduction, p. xi.
35. Ibid., T-M. 24; Introduction, p. xii.
36. Lou Sebock (ed.), *Netherlands Atlases*, op. cit., Introduction, p. xii.
37. Susan Gole, *A Series*, op. cit., T-M. 20-1.
38. Ibid., T-M. 15.
39. Ibid., T-M. 19.
40. Ibid., T-M. 15; R.H. Phillimore, op. cit., vol. I, p. 209.
41. R.H. Phillimore, op. cit., vol. I, p. 209.
42. Susan Gole, *A Series*, op. cit., M. 25, 26.

43. Ibid., T-M. 20, 21.
44. Ibid., T-M. 20; Susan Gole, *India Within*, op. cit., pp. 61, 64.
45. Ibid., T-M. 20.
46. Ibid., T-M. 21.
47. Susan Gole, *India Within*, op. cit., p. 60.
48. Ibid., p. 60.
49. R.H. Phillimore, op. cit., vol. I, p. 71.

CHAPTER 4

Changing Perspectives and Perceptions

The eighteenth century, spilling over to the nineteenth century saw a major change in the political scenario in India, resulting in more avenues of getting empirical geographical data for the Western map-makers. Conflicts began to erupt between Europeans and Indian rulers and among the Europeans themselves. On the other hand, Europeans had begun settling down in India for good, although the change was initially slow, but was surely coming, and they knew it. By the end of the eighteenth century the decision was finally made, as the English came out victorious, and subsequently established the greatest empire the world has ever seen. During the innumerable wars in the subcontinent, their military marched to almost every corner of the country, and nobody could dare to stop it carrying route-surveys, the forerunners of the detailed topographical and other surveys. This was made all the more easy with the advance in survey methodology, techniques, and instrumentation. It gave the Europeans, especially the English, ample opportunities to survey at leisure, and thus India began to be geographically thrown open to the world. Its national boundaries were almost drawn up and most of the major rivers, their sources and broad courses recognized and laid down on maps. Even a casual map-maker now had to use now the easily available empirical geographical information for his maps. This helped to conclusively eliminate, in due course, the geographical myths and absurdities from the early maps of India.

We now know that till the eighteenth century, there was little real knowledge about the geography of India available to map-makers in the West. No map publisher ever claimed his map to be based on purely empirical data. The maps published thus far in Italy, Holland, France, England and other centres were based less on classical tradition and more on fables. Fantastic and inaccurate geographical information were spread by individual missionaries, navigators, mariners and travellers. Although there were not many avenues of cross-checking the data used by the early map-makers and their publishers, it seems, the map-makers deliberately avoided selecting empirical data, and did not search for the classical information, waiting to be discovered. They preferred to borrow and copy from one another, and adding a few variations and details as their fancy dictated.

Herman Moll (d. 1732) was the first map-maker of the eighteenth century who copied the controversials in his 1701 map.[1] He might have been aware of the inaccuracies, since these were being seen in maps since very early in the history of map-making. Moll's map shows the river Indus, the ancient 'western boundary' of India, coming out at about

39° latitude, flowing almost straight south-southwest to the sea. River Ganges comes out from beyond the K-2 range, from about 105° east longitude (calculated from which prime-meridian is not stated), and flows mostly around that longitude, down south to the Bay of Bengal. It meets the Bay at the coordinates 23° north latitude and 106° east longitude. River Guenga, the 'Ganga' of the south, is also there on the map, coming out of a place about 18° north latitude, flowing northeast till about 100° east longitude, moving eastward, but always remaining south of the Tropic of Cancer, till it meets the Bay of Bengal. Like the 'tradition' of the day, mythical lake 'Chimay' is also there on the map, shown at a place southeast of Ava, but marked below 'Tibet', between approximate latitudes of 34° north and 36° north, and longitudes of 114° east and 117° east. The western-most river (not named) coming out of the lake is shown meeting the eastern-most channel of the delta of the Ganges, before flowing into the Bay.

Almost a quarter century later, Moll was still adhering to the same ideas. In 1722, in his work entitled *A Complete System Geography, Ancient and Modern*,[2] which contained 31 maps, only 2 maps were of India. The first map was entitled 'The West Part of India', or the 'Empire of the Great Mogul 1712' (Map 4.2).[3] It covered the territory from Kabul to Pegu, and from the Maldives Islands to Kashmir. Here, the Ganges is shown flowing directly south from an unnamed lake. Another point worth mentioning is that the Brahmaputra River is shown coming from the east through Assam, and the Tsangpo is not marked at all. Like others, Moll, after so many years in the business, still believed in the existence of the southern 'Guenga', and had clearly marked it on his map. The second map on India in the book, entitled, 'The East Part of India Beyond the River Ganges (1729)' (Map 4.4),[4] covered the Andaman and Nicobar Islands, and Sumatra, and the eastern part of the Indian mainland. The map shows 'Asem or Acham' (Assam), and the Laquia River flowing westward from 'Chaammay' (Chiamay) Lake. Thus, we see that Herman Moll carried all the three fallacies under our study throughout his mapping career.

Eighteenth century offered greater opportunities for counter-checking and investigating the available cartographic and geographic materials on India, but the apparent tendency of the map-makers was to ignore them as their predecessors had done in the earlier centuries. Out of a dozen or so popular map-markers mentioned below who followed Moll only a few can be counted as seemingly ahead of the rest in their speculations, and appeared to have some understanding of the current geographical puzzles and mysteries surrounding the theme of our story. The majority of cartographers till the mid-eighteenth century just followed the old oft-beaten track. Majority of them were either publishers or printers, and not geographers[5] in the true sense. They had no basic qualifications and aptitude to be considered scientific map-makers; they were just businessmen-publishers.

We may look very briefly, at the map-making activities of some cartographers:

1. Nicolas de Fer[6] (1646-1720) though a prolific map-maker, was considered an ordinary geographer;
2. Frederick de Wit[7] and family (father, 1613-1706, son d. 1710) were publishers;
3. Henry Abraham Chatelain[8] (1684-1743) (Map 4.1) was a knowledgeable map-maker; his maps in many ways were an improvement over the earlier maps of the period; was

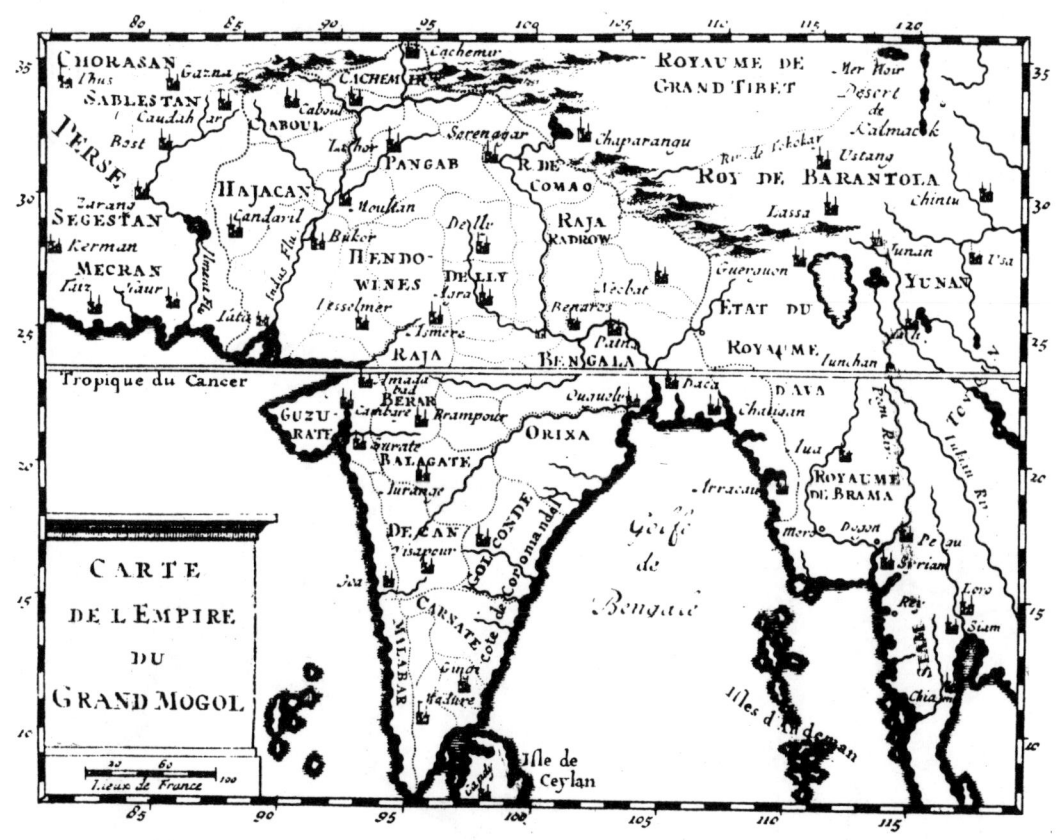

Map 4.1: *Geneologie des Empereurs Mogols* by Henri Abraham Chatelain (1699).

the author of a popular atlas *Atlas historique* (1719); also of small book, in several volumes, wherein 'all the information supposedly necessary for a well-read gentleman at court' was incorporated;

4. Guillaume de L'Isle[9] (1675-1726) (Map 4.3); was a well-known and respected cartographer; became the *Premier Geographe* at an early age; began drawing maps since the age of eight; maintained a wide correspondence throughout his life with many reputed geographers and map-makers of the day; his maps were included by many cartographers in their atlases;

5. Jean Nicolas Bellin[10] (1703-72) (Maps 4.6, 4.8) was attached to the French Marine Office was an industrious cartographer;

6. J.B.B. d'Anville[11] (1697-1782) (Map 4.5) was the official cartographer for the French East India Company; his other activities are given later in chapter;

7. G.R. de Vaugondy[12] and family (1688-1766) (Maps 4.7.1-4.7.5) were a popular map-makers at the French court; Vaugondy's *Atlas Universel* (1757) was engraved by a well-known artist. He was well-informed of Indian geography;

8. Robert Bonne's[13] (1729-94) (Map 4.9) *Atlas Moderne* was well received by the readers; his maps of India were used by other map-makers in their works;

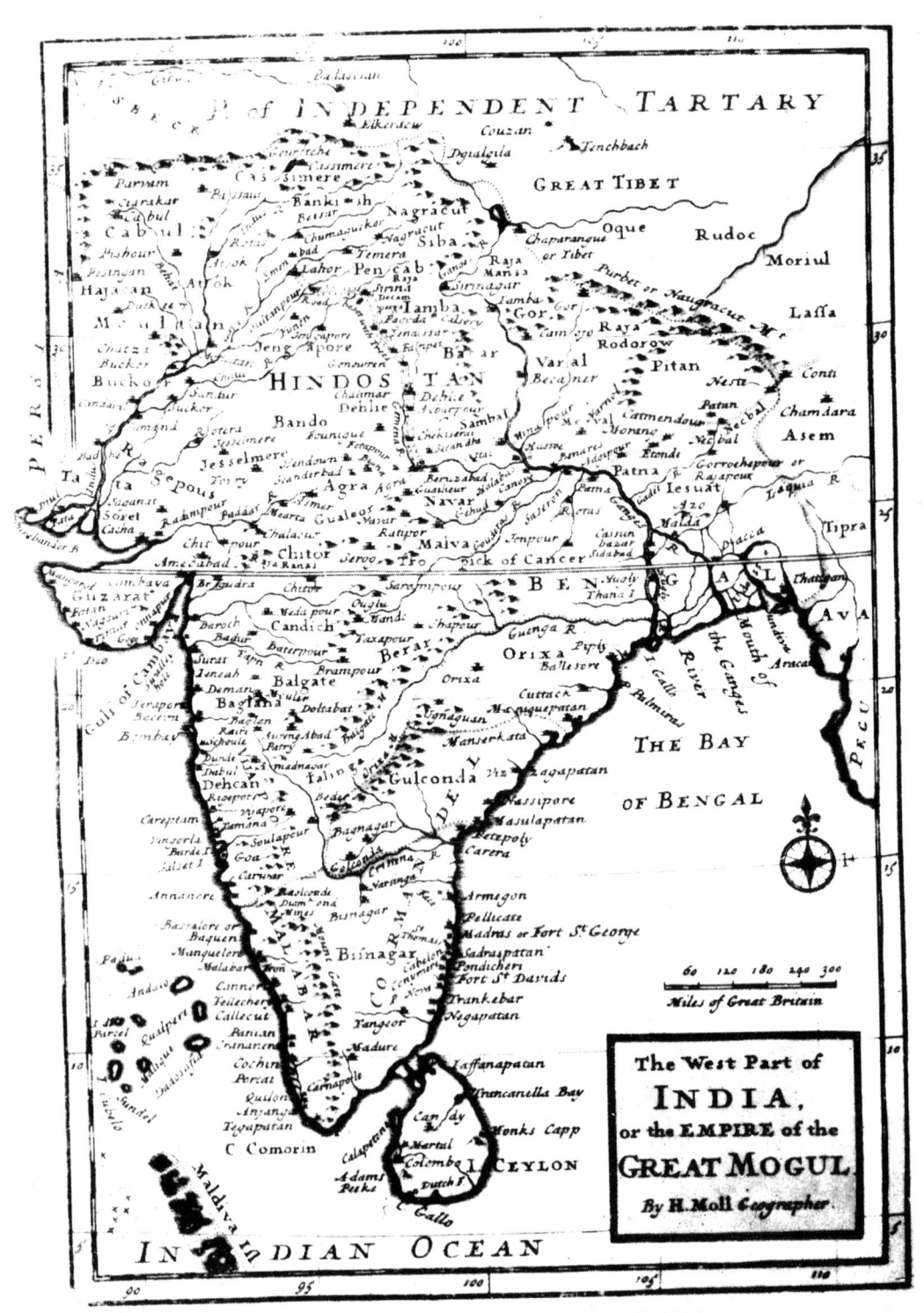

Map 4.2: *The West Part of India* by Herman Moll (1712).

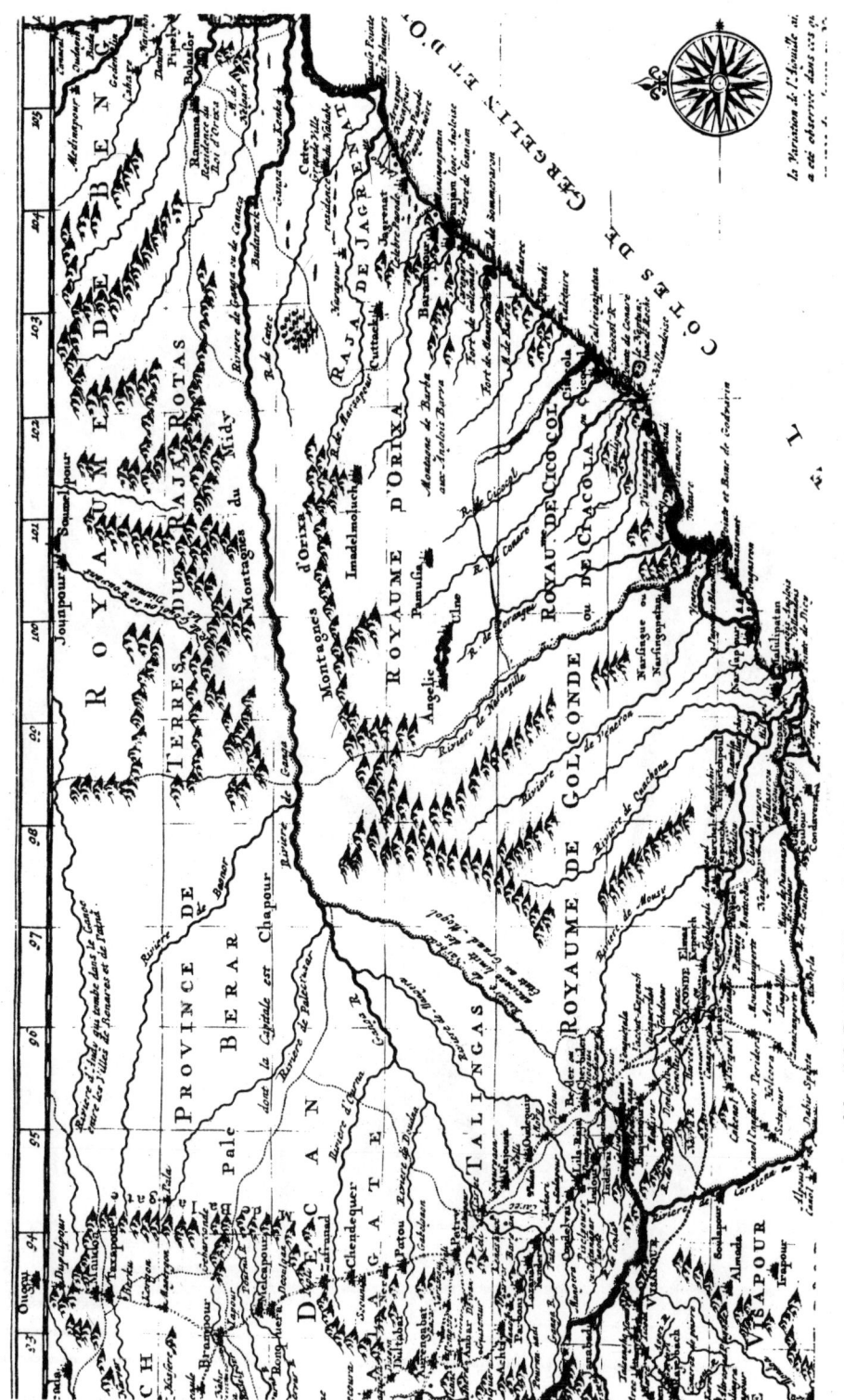

Map 4.3: Detail of *Cartes des Cotes de Malabar et de Coromandel* by Guillaume de L'Isle, (1722).

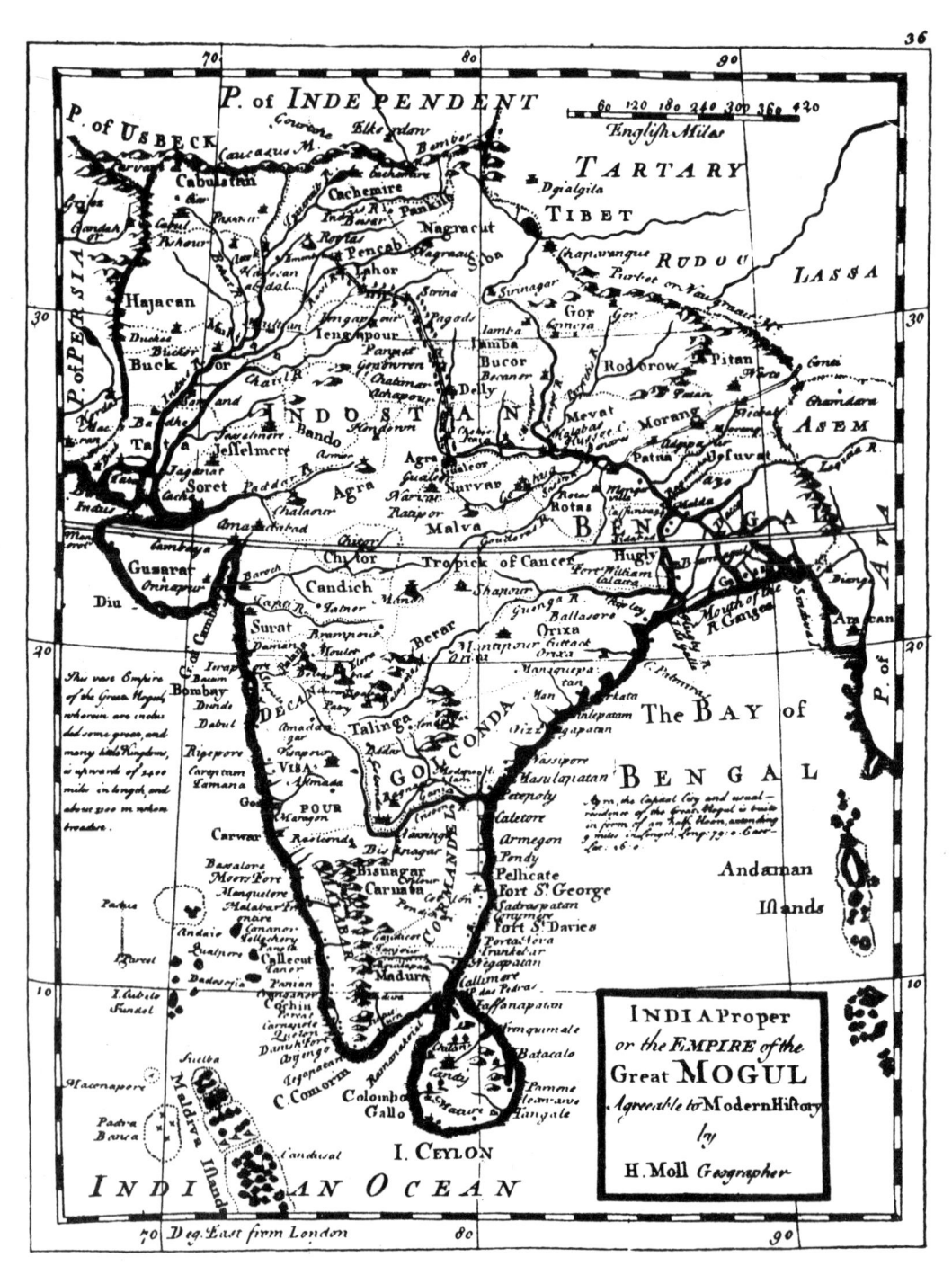

Map 4.4: *India Proper* by Herman Moll (1729).

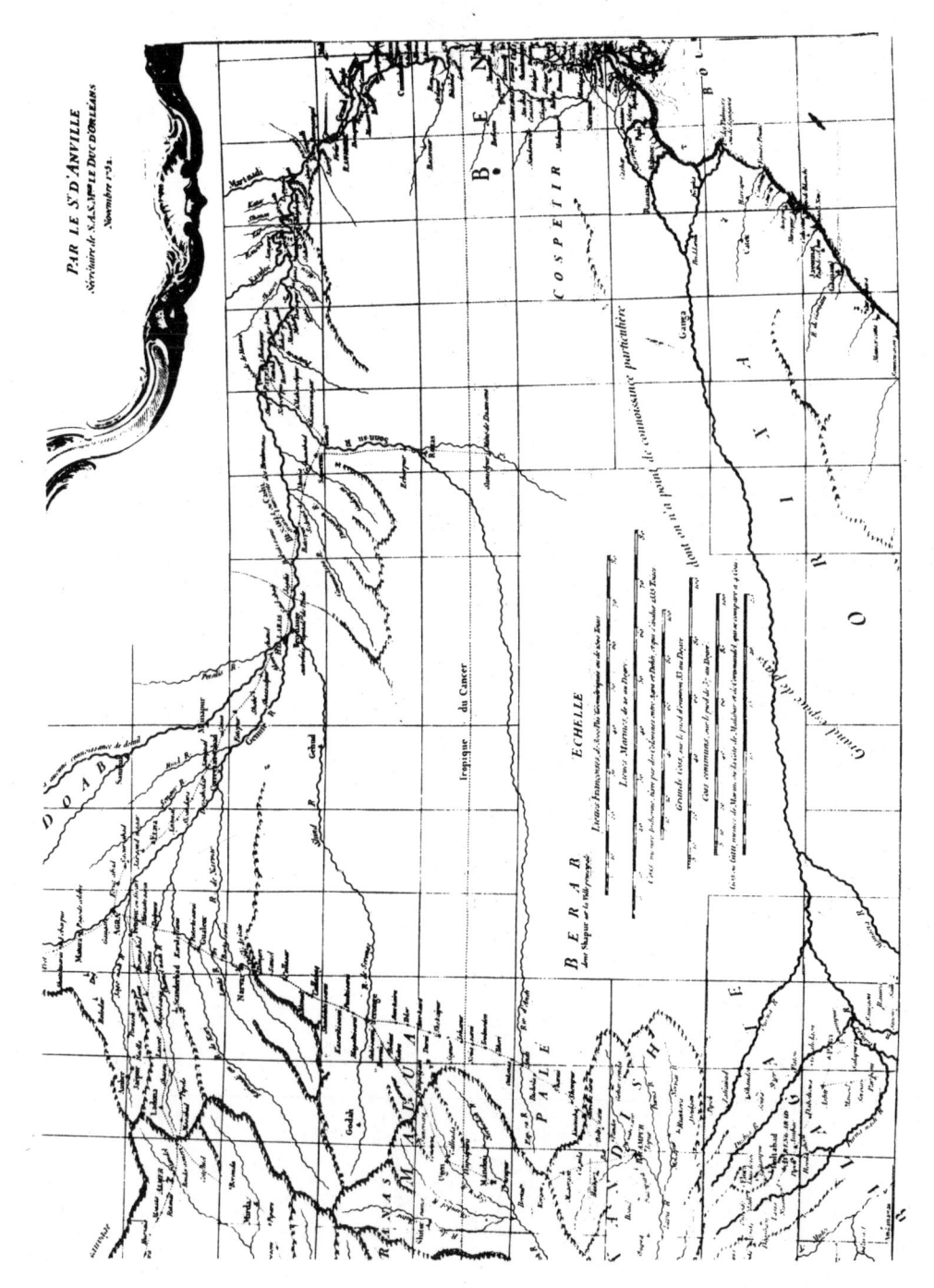

Map 4.5: Detail of *Carte de L'Inde* by Jean Baptiste Bourguignon d'Anville (1752).

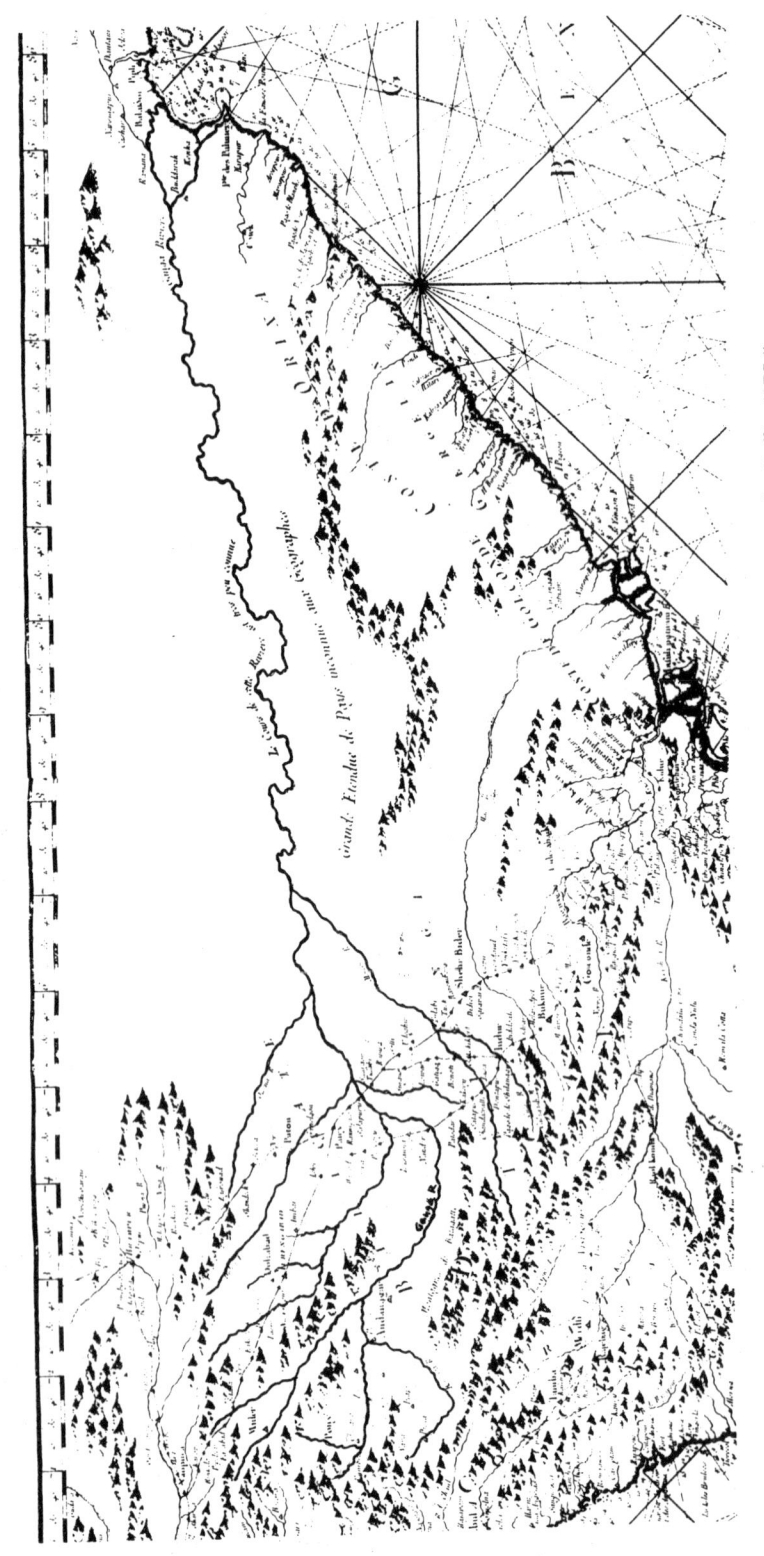

Map 4.6: Detail of *Carte Reduite de la Presqu' Isle de L'Inde* by Jean Nicolas Bellin (1756).

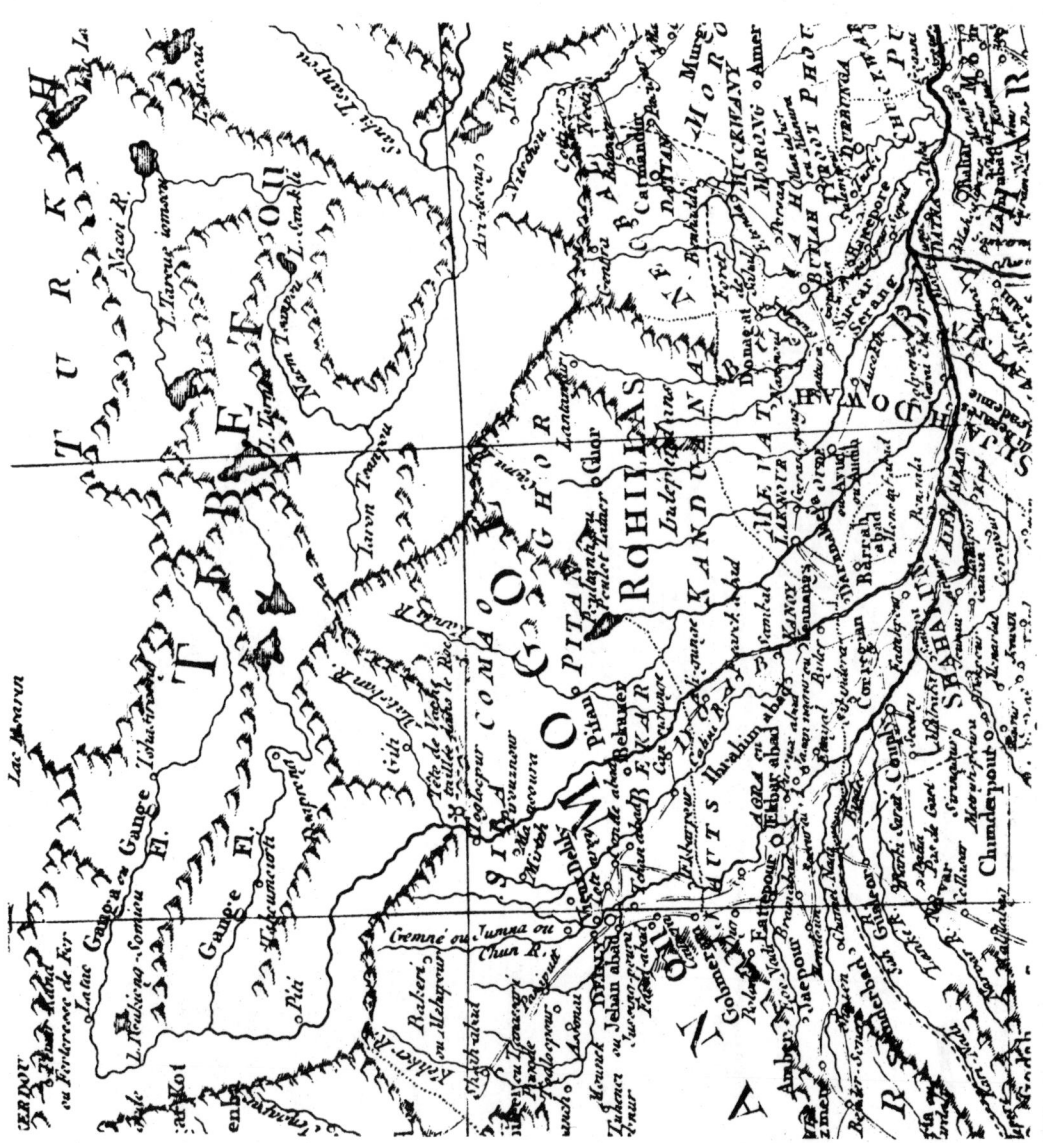

Map 4.7.1: Detail of Presqu' Isle des Indes Orientales (N-E) by G. Robert de Vaugondy (1758).

Map 4.7.2: Detail of *Presqu' Isle des Indes Orientales* (N-W) by G. Robert de Vaugondy (1758).

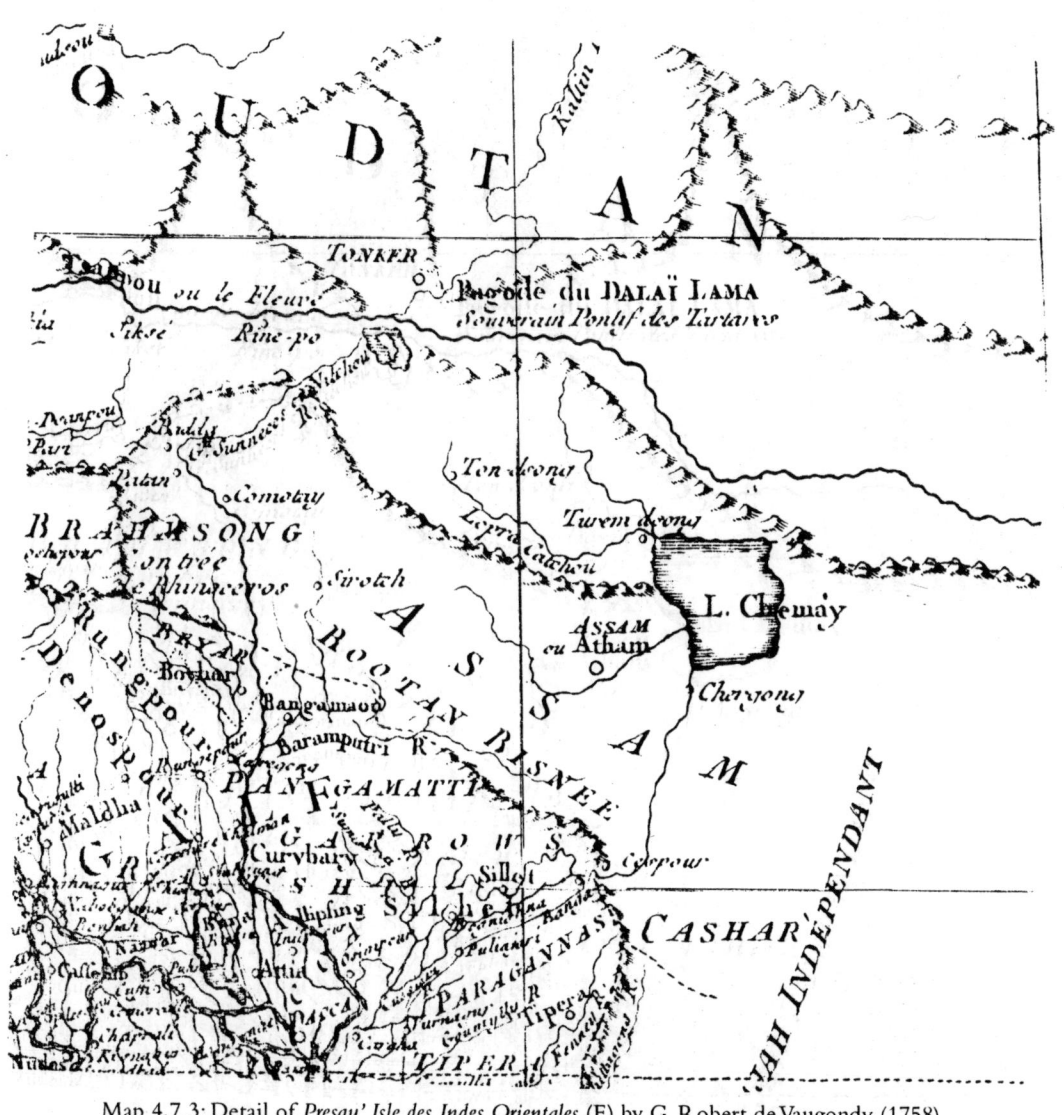

Map 4.7.3: Detail of *Presqu' Isle des Indes Orientales* (E) by G. Robert de Vaugondy (1758).

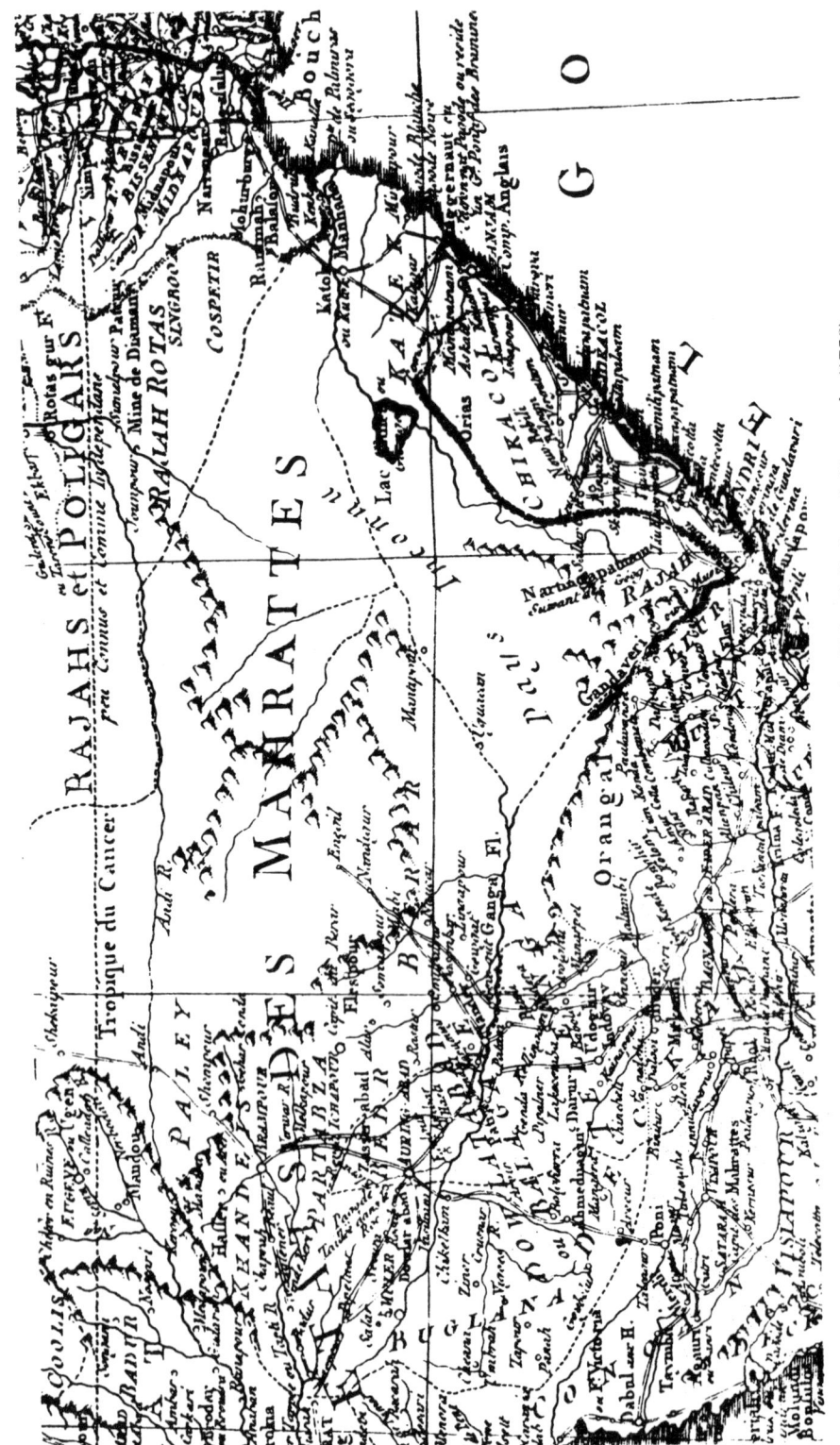

Map 4.7.4: Detail of *Presqu' Isle des Indes Orientales* (S) by G. Robert de Vaugondy (1758).

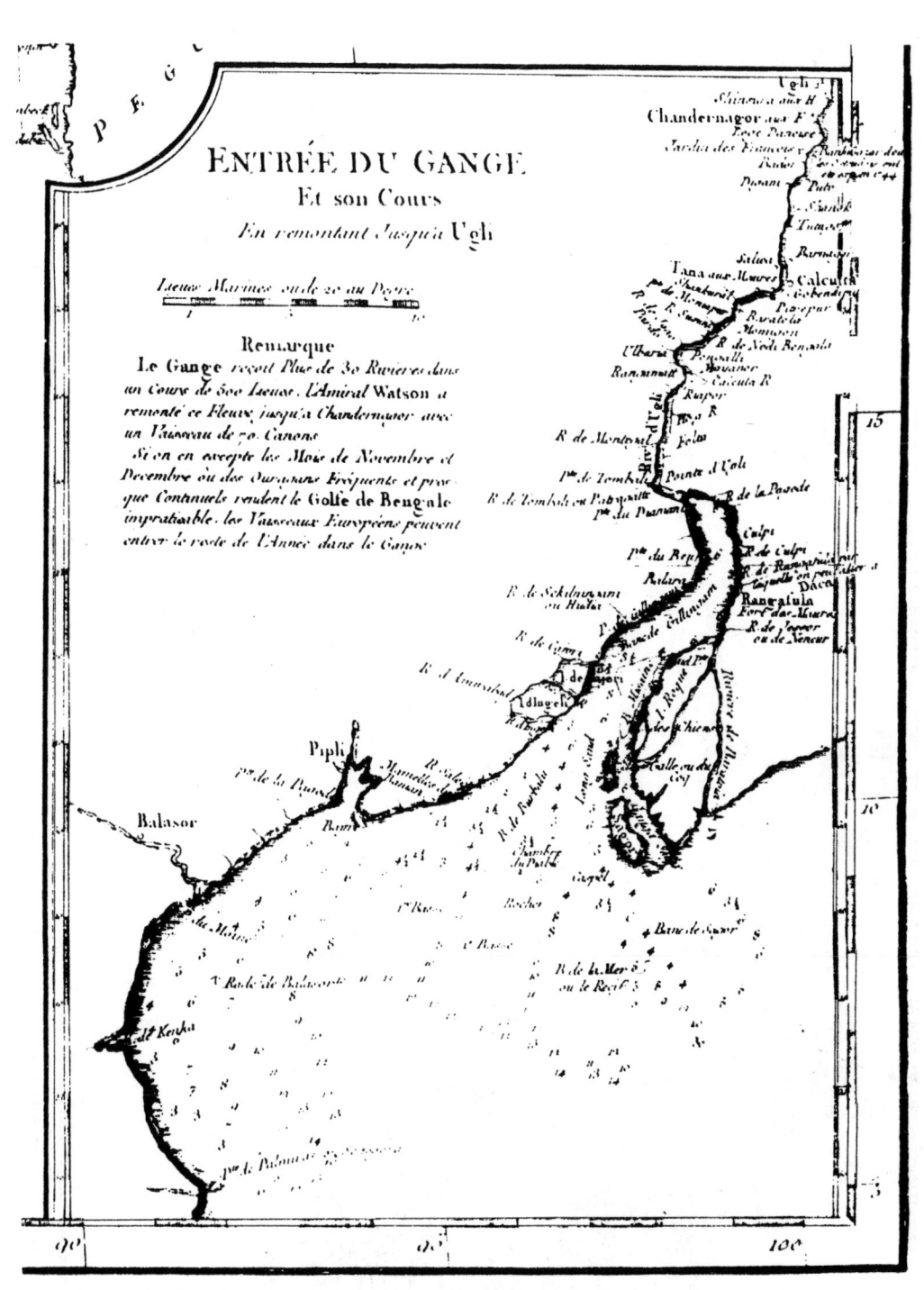

Map 4.7.5: Detail of *Presqu' Isle des Indes Orientales* (inset) by G. Robert de Vaugondy (1758).

Map 4.8: *Carte de L'Indoustan* by Jean Nicolas Bellin (1763).

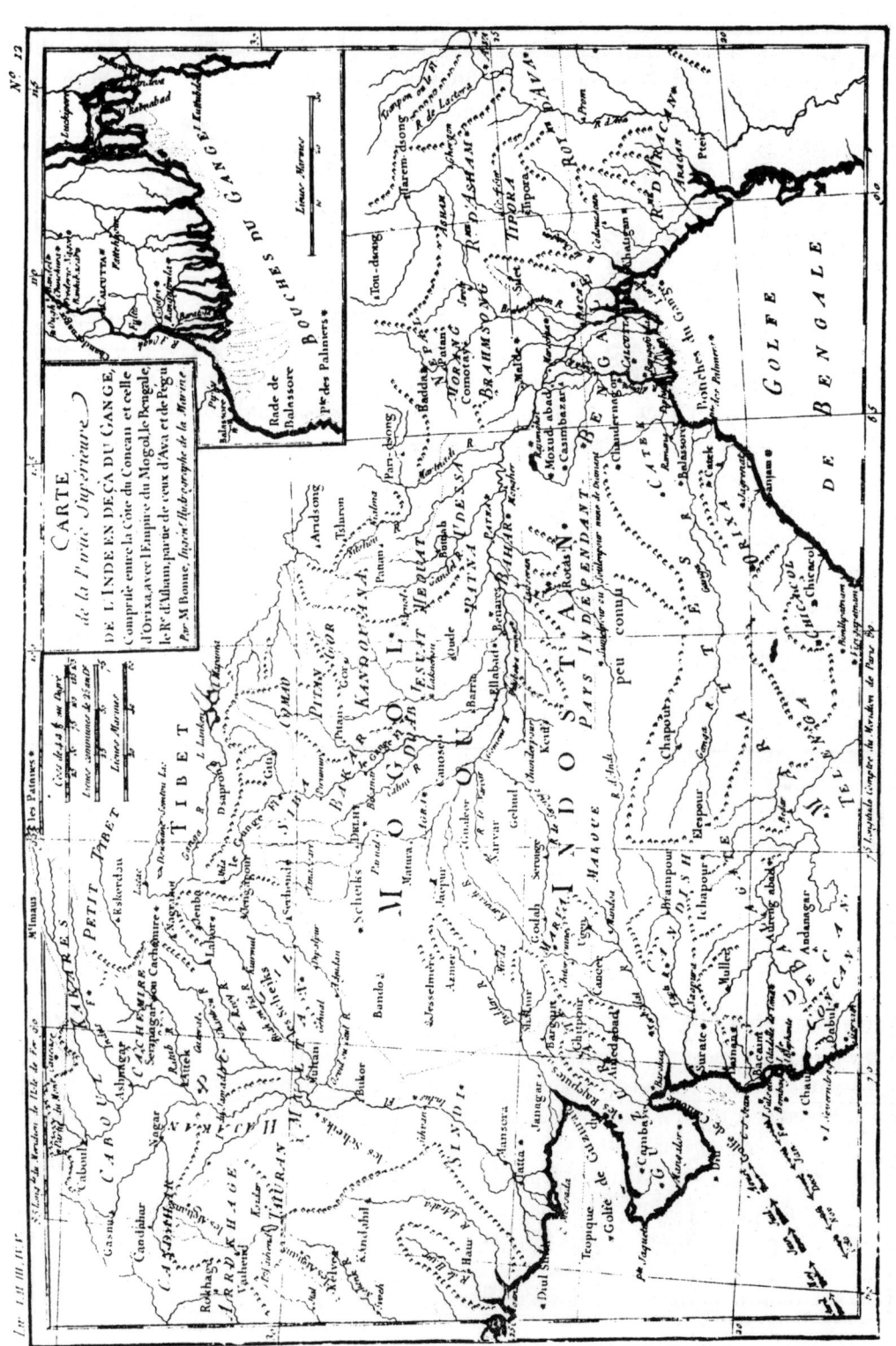

Map 4.9: Carte de la Parie Superieure de L'Inde by Robert Bonne (1771).

9. Thomas Jefferys[14] (d. 1771) (Maps 4.10.1-4.10.3); was a bookseller and a publisher; his map of India (1768) became very popular, with many editions being printed. They were used by many famous map-publishers in their atlases; more information about his mapping activity is given later in the chapter.
10. James Rennell[15] (1742-1830) is called the Father of Indian Cartography. He was Surveyor General of Bengal in 1767; he had vast experience of field surveys and had unrestricted access to all the cartographical and geographical material lodged with the British East India Company in India and England. His mapping activities are mentioned further in this chapter;
11. de la Rochette's[16] (1731-1802) (Maps 4.11.1-4.11.3); was a respected map-maker; his maps were generally published by one of the best map publishers, William Faden; de la Richette is some of the known cartographers who was active on the scene publishing maps of India. Though all the maps tell the same story about India, the maps of at least four of these map-makers of the latter half of the eighteenth century show a different tinge. These are de Vaugondy's (1758), Jefferys' (1768, 1794), Rennell's (1782, 1793), and de la Rochette's (1788). They were ahead of the rest in their geographical interpretation of the Indian scenario.

The gist of the investigation of the subject so far is that most maps continued to show the myths and fantasies generated in the post-Greek classical period, the medieval fantasies carried through the description of the 'paradise' of Marco Polo, the storms and the resultant confusion created by Ptolemy in Europe since the fifteenth century onwards, and the fabulous saga of 'travel literature' by de Barros.

Significantly, there appeared in 1717 a special map dealing with the source of the Ganges. It is generally known as Lamas' map of Tibet.[17] The story behind its preparation and publication, is interesting. In the very early years of the eighteenth century, Emperor Kanghi of China wanted Father Jean Baptiste Regis, who joined the Jesuit Mission in Peking in 1698,[18] to compile a map of his empire based on the European method of surveying. For this purpose, the Emperor selected two Lamas who were specially trained for the job. They were dispatched[19] 'to Tibet with orders to draw accurate maps of that country as far west as the Ganges. Their expedition was so far successful that they reached Lanka-Dhe (the Rakas Lake, situated west of Manasarovar lake). They learned from the Lamas of a local monastery, that the Ganges had its origin in that lake. However, before they were able to take latitudes of the Lanka-Dhe region ... the two Lamas had to flee from the country.'[20] 'The result of this half-hearted attempt was, that the Lamas' map, showing the Ganges issuing from Lanka-Dhe, was accepted as correct.'[21.] Even though, according to Rennell, this Lamas' map was inaccurate, it had to be accepted as it was for the first map of this region. It gives a fair idea of the upper gorges of the rivers in the area, and seemingly, there was no other authority for these regions.

The publication of this map brings to the fore the earlier speculations about the origin of the much venerated river Ganga, Gangai or Ganges. The later cartographers were reminded of the early efforts of the map-makers, and their publications brought in different perceptions about the most important river of India. Thus, the early inaccuracies were now turned into competitive controversial fallacies. A number of travellers, writers and geographers together with the map-makers turned their attention to this geographical problem, and quite a few map-makers later came up illustrating various versions of this region, of the river Ganges and its upper course.

Another map that created a stir was a 1752 map of India by the celebrated French cartographer, Jean Baptiste Bourgignon D'Anville (Map 4.5),[22] better known as the geographer to the French East India Company. Although it is said that he 'largely rescued the geography of India from the vagaries of fancy',[23] he himself fell a victim to the fallacies under discussion, and being perpetuated since about two centuries by every map-maker in the Western world. He included one of these inaccuracies in his famous map of India of 1752—the southern 'Ganga'.

Examination of D'Anville's map *Carte de L'Inde*[24] (Map 4.6) indicates that in the north, the map does not cover the area of the source of the Ganges. It only shows the upper courses of the rivers 'Gange' (Ganges), 'Gemne' (Jumna) and their tributaries in the region from about 30° latitude, the area covered by about 92° 30' and 96° east longitude (from Paris). Except for showing the upper courses of the rivers and a few place-names, nothing else is marked. In the east, the area where the lake 'Chiamay' is generally shown by other map-makers, is left blank. But the southern river 'Ganga' is shown prominently flowing with its tributaries in the upper region of western India. Its central course remains generally between latitudes of 20° and 21°, below the Tropic of Cancer. The entire length, including the tributaries, is covered between approximate longitudes of 90° and 100° east.

What his compulsions were in using the data he used, have not been specifically explained. This is typical of the attitude of the known map-makers till about the last quarter of the eighteenth century.

Praising d'Anville's judicious nature of selection of material William Herbert said that: 'He adjusted his map to all astronomical positions he could collect, and then built up the detail of coast-line and interior from any records he could find, discussing positions and distances given by writers even as early as Ptolemy and the Arab geographers, and hardly overlooking any possible source of information.'[25] He further explained 'When it is considered that this excellent geographer had scarcely any materials to work on for the inland parts of India but some vague itineraries and books of travels, one is really astonished to find them so well described as they are.'[26] . . . About D'Anville's methodology of map making, Herbert wrote:'He left the unknown heart of India almost blank, and from the section which covers Bengal it will be seen how conscientious he was to avoid filling up blanks with imaginary detail, though he did follow the crowd in accepting the fabulous river Ganga.'[27] Why? About the Ganges and its upper course, Herbert mentions that D'Anville has not come up well, and records 'an almost total defect of intelligence concerning the course of the Ganges, from its entrance into India, to its reception of the Jomanes (Jumna conflux), and his map does not show anything to the north of the Ganges except 'the points of junction of the larger tributaries, giving no indication whatever of any mountains'.[28]

A contemporary historian, Robert Orme in 1778 wrote about his own depiction of the peninsular 'Ganga' in the General Map of India. A note in his handwriting on the proof copy of the map states: 'The Ganga, running thro' Berar and falling at Balasore is from Mr. D'Anville's notion which we have now every reason to believe wrong.'[29] Later, the reputed geographer, H.R. Mill, states: 'The uncritical study of Asia and Africa by D'Anville had recently purged the maps of those continents of all their traditional details as regards rivers, lakes and mountains, and left only the coastlines and such features of the interior as had been seen by European travellers of repute. Little was left in Central Asia, and practically nothing of Africa.'[30]

It is surprising that such a reputed cartographer would 'follow the Crowd', and would not express or indicate his opposition to the depiction of these fallacies, as in other instances, by avoiding to elucidate them in any manner, or boycotting them altogether.

There is another seemingly authentic contemporary empirical source in the last quarter of the eighteenth century which discards the theory of the existence of the southern 'Ganga'. On 28 February 1778, Ritchie, the official hydrographical surveyor of the British East India Company, sent in his report of the survey of Point Palmyras, False Point, and part of Orissa coast, describing the geographical features, tidal waves, and their effect on the navigation in this part of the Bay of Bengal, and similar other navigational hazards in the area, to the Bengal Council for onward transmission to the Directors in England.[31] The report was a detailed one of Palmyras Point made 'to fix a proper spot for a light-house' and 'he is pretty certain that no large river (by the name of Ganga) falls in between Pt. Palmyras'. This demolishes all the English views so far as the existence of the mythical Ganga River.[32] The writings, reports, travel records, field books, memoirs, and even maps of English surveyors attached with the armies marching through the region confirm the non-existence of the mythical river Ganga in peninsular India. The traverses of Charles Reynolds from Surat to Poona via Hyderabad and from Nagpur to Agra (1788, 1792-3); Thomas Enbury and James Blunt from Hyderabad to Kalpi (1792-3) and James Blunt from Chunar to Rajahmundry (1795), etc.,[33] also make no mention of the southern Ganga.

During the latter half of the eighteenth century, all the three main fallacies began to fall apart. This happened chiefly because of the information gathered on the battlefields, which began to slowly filter down to the map-makers of the time.

With the increase in opportunities of for social interaction with the people of India during this century, militarily and otherwise, and the greater involvement of governmental agencies through their trade-companions, reliable geographical information was more readily available than before. Maps of cartographers like Guillaume de l'Isle (1675-1726) (Map 4.3), J.B.B. d'Anville (1697-1782) (Map 4.5), G.R. de Vaugondy (1688-1766) (Maps 4.7.1-4.7.5), Thomas Jefferys (d. 1771) (Maps 4.10.1-4.10.3) were in great demand for updating maps. This was because of their contacts with the authorities and other official agencies.

With the coming of Lamas' map of Tibet of 1717, and later, the popularity of D'Anville's map of 1752, the well-known cartographers of the day began to take more interest in India's geography.

Gilbert Robert de Vaugondy, and his family, were popular map-makers at the French court.[34] His map, entitled *Presqu 'Isle des Indes Orientales* (1758) (Maps 4.7.1-4.7.5) was studied by the then geographers with keen eyes. The map covers the within approximate

5° north latitude and 35° east latitude, to about 55° east and 115° east longitude (from the prime meridien of Paris). The river Ganges is marked with its two upper branches coming from the east (Map 4.7.1). Both are named 'Ganga or Gange'. After meeting at an unnamed place, the river flows southward till Piti, and then moves towards a place, also unnamed, that could be Hardwar.

De Vaugondy has also shown lake Chemay (Chiamay) (Map 4.7.3) in the far northeast of Assam. The shape of this lake, as shown on the map, is almost rectangular, with four sharp angles. Its location is marked by approximate 26° 30' degrees latitude, and 111° and 112° 30' longitude, east of Paris. Fort Tarem Dzon is situated at the northeast corner of the lake. The map also shows Tsangpo River, which other maps of the period did not mark. It is shown passing north of lake Chamay from east to west, but not far north of it. It does not enter the lake (no river is shown entering the lake). No river is marked even entering India in this region from the east.

De Vaugondy's 'Ganga' in the south (Map 4.7.4) issues out just east of Surat, flowing southeast till about 19° latitude and 77° longitude. Here, it bifurcates and the northern branch moves in the northeast direction. From this point onwards, the river course is perhaps, conjectural, as it is marked in a broken or dotted line, a feature not used by other map-makers. The river reaches north of 'Chilka or Ganga' Lake, and meets the Manhada River coming out of the lake, then reaches the Bay of Bengal at Palmyras Point. The southern branch of the main river is named 'Gaudaveri or Muri R' (Godavari River). This flows southeastward and joins the Bay of Bengal.

But unlike D'Anville, it appears de Vaugondy was not sure of the course of the 'Ganga', as he marked the course of the river in dotted lines—surely an advance in the true evaluation of the then current practice and information.

De Vaugondy also included an inset map (Map 4.7.5) in his map of India. This inset map covers the portion from Hooghly town to the north-west coast of the Bay of Bengal to the south of Point Palmyras. This little map shows entrypoints of many rivers, small and large, from the west. Though some are named, river Ganga of the south is not mentioned anywhere near the town of Balasore. This fact indicates that unlike others, de Vaugondy did not seriously believe in the existence of the southern Ganga.

Over a decade later, in 1768, another cartographer who was 'Geographer to the King',[35] Englishman Thomas Jefferys, published a map entitled *The East Indies, with the Roads* (Maps 4.10.1-4.10.3). The map was engraved by Robert Sayer in 1789, and contained 'additions and emendations from actual surveys made by James Rennell, the Geographer to the British East India Company.'[36] The map was published posthumously in May 1794 and is discussed later. Jefferys died in 1774. It may be noted that this map was initially published by Laurie & Whittle as part of their atlas in 1794 along with its earlier versions.

In 1768, before learning of Rennell's views on the source of the river Ganges, Jefferys did not show the exact place of the origin of the river on his earlier edition. He did, however, describe a place in the Siba region as 'A Cow cut in the rocks' (Map 4.10.1). The river is shown southward. This indicates Jafferys' adherence in his earlier map-making career to the traditional depiction of mystical fantasies.

In that very year, he wrote a letter to the Court of Directors of the East India Company in England for permission to use the geographical and cartographic material of James Rennell in the company's custody in London. It appears the permission came after Jeffrey's death. The publisher who brought out the map posthumously in 1794,[37] however, incorporated the new information and the views of Rennell into the map. How far this information changed his earlier views, and, after a gap of a quarter of a century in the business of map-making, what were his views by the time the permission came, cannot be ascertained at this stage. But the final map of 1794 seems to be fine augury.

More than two centuries after the fallacies about India started creeping into cartographic literature, some map-makers seriously began to repudiate them by 'showing' their dissent in their maps. Thomas Jefferey's was one of them. Close examination of his 1768 map of India entitled *The East Indies with the Roads* shows that his southern 'Ganga' is very much different[38] (Map 4.10.1-4.10.3). The river shown in the central India region, flowing towards northeast and drawn in double dotted lines, indicating thereby that he was not convinced of its course in that territory. On the other hand, he showed the upper course of the river together with its flow in its last legs in bold lines, as he seemed to be sure of its delineation in these regions. It is also significant that he did not name this large river anywhere throughout its vast course. However, in its last stage, after its confluence with another large river coming from northwest, passing through the 'Chilka or Ganga Lake', the combined river is named as 'Manhada' River (Mahanadi?), just before it is shown falling into the Bay of Bengal. The upper tributaries of this unnamed river, 'Muler', 'Crushuar', and 'Benhera' are, however, clearly delineated and named.

The outline of the lake 'Chemay' (Map 4.10.2) is not drawn in bold lines, as in other parts on the map; instead it is marked in broken lines, as Jeffrey's was not sure of its existence or location. To make his intention more clear he has written inside the lake, 'The supposed Situation of Chemay Lake', which clearly spells out his doubts. The north and the east of the lake, is surrounded by 'Dsirih' mountains and its off-shoots. Most of these run in north-south direction. No river is marked penetrating them, although a number of small rivers, not named, are seen flowing into the lake from the southern and western watershed of these ranges. River Lakia is, however, the only one marked, seen coming out of the lake and flowing towards Assam in the west.

The above confirms that the cartographic views of Thomas Jefferys on the 'inaccuracies' under discussion were radically different to those of the 'crowd', who were diligently following the old maps in this regard since more than two centuries.

In 1782, James Rennell, the 'Father of Indian Cartography', published his *Map of Hindoostan*.[39] About this map, he says, 'I have been enabled by means of observations of Longitude taken at Bombay, Cochin, Madras, Calcutta, Agra, etc., together with measured lines and surveys extended from the above places, to frame a very good groundwork for my map....'[40]

In this map Rennell does not show lake 'Chiamay' in northeastern India, nor does he depict the southern 'Ganga'. From the east of northern part of the Western Ghats, because of the topography of the Central India plateau, all the rivers flow, unlike the course of the 'Ganga' in other maps, in the south-east direction.

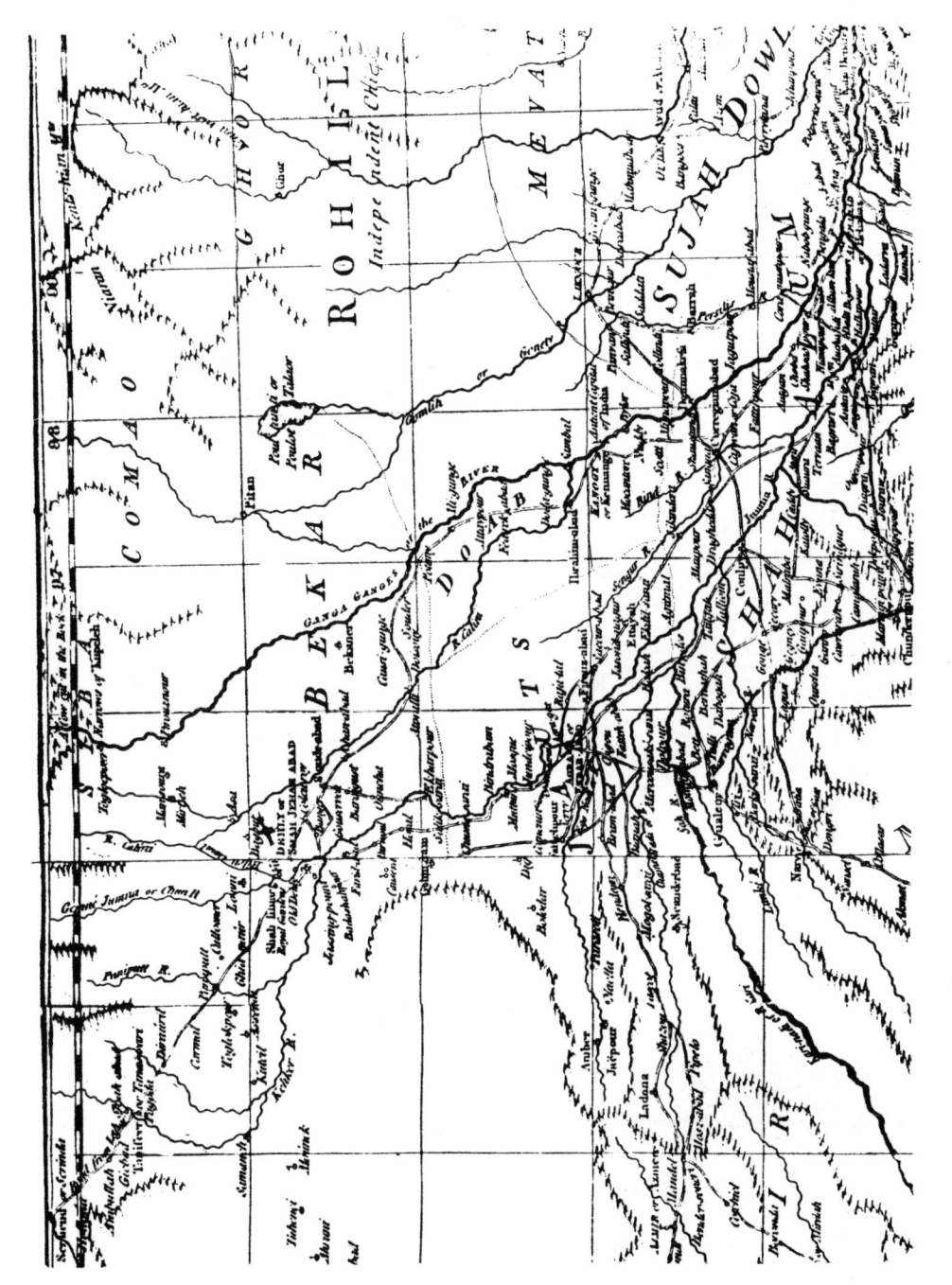

Map 4.10.1: Detail of *The East Indies with the Roads* (N) by Thomas Jefferys (1768).

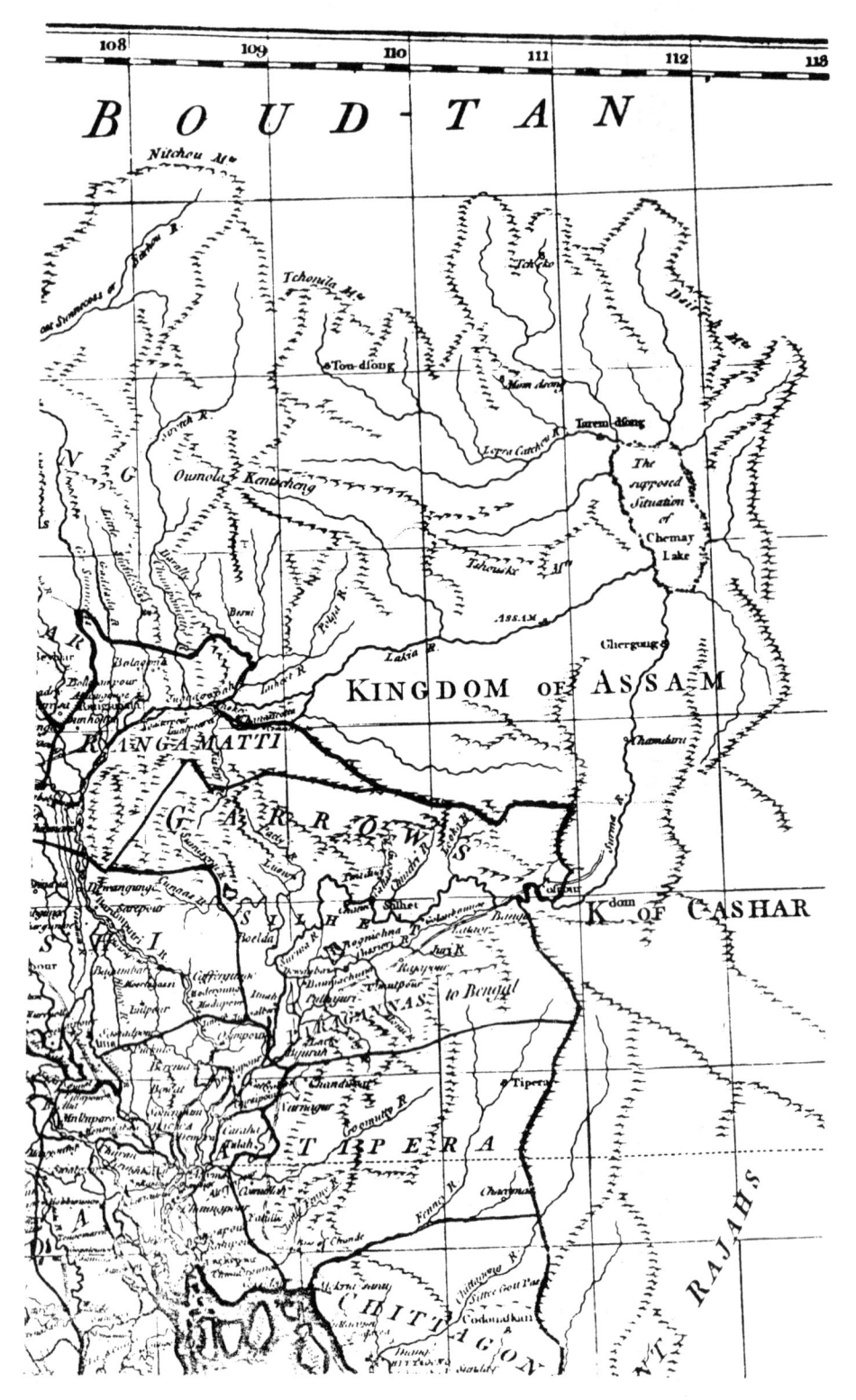

Map 4.10.2: Detail of *The East Indies with the Roads* (E) by Thomas Jefferys (1768).

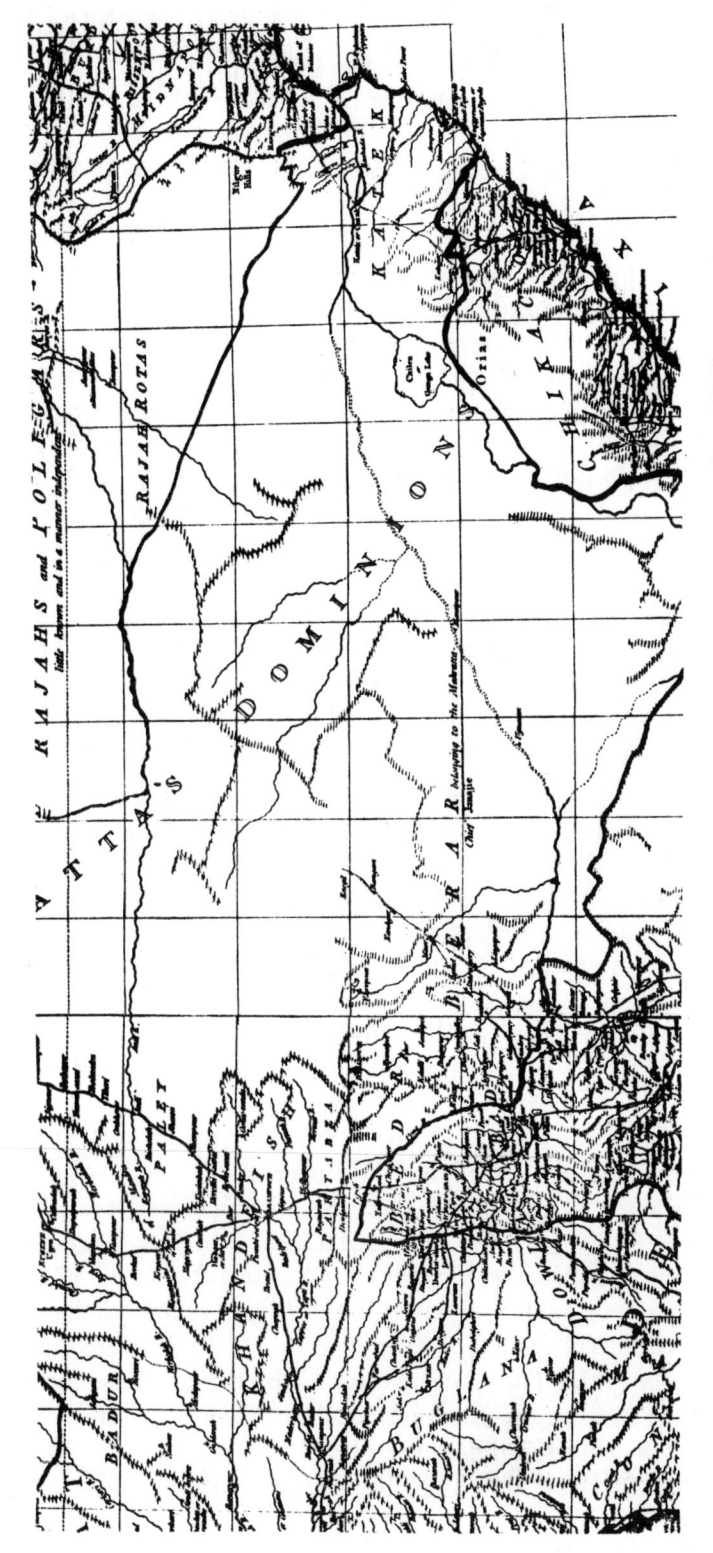

Map 4.10.3: Detail of *The East Indies with the Roads* (S) by Thomas Jefferys (1768).

In compiling his map of 1782, Rennell, like D'Anville, followed the method of close analysis of all the early historical and geographical material available. He had accumulated an abundance of them, collected by him, by the English surveyors for the last 25 years, and by others. This map was accompanied by a memoir explaining its construction like that by D'Anville. Although he had an advantage of huge store of material, 'wide areas were still completely blank, or dependent on the journals of casual travelers. . .'.[41] In 1785, just three years after the first edition the memoir was revised,[42] and, Rennell included therein his *Account of the Ganges and Brahmaputra Rivers*.[43]

Another map with a difference was that by L.S. de la Rochette, a compiler, his map *Hind, Hindoostan or India* (Maps 4.11.1-4.11.3), was published by one of the renowned map publishers, William Faden, Geographer to the King, in 1788. Before examining the map, it would help in our evaluation, if we first look at the 'advertisement' printed in the map's bottom left corner. It reads: 'For the new and interesting particulars with which this map is enriched, especially in the northern parts, we are chiefly indebted to the Geographical Description of, Father Joseph Tienffenthaller, Apostolic Missionary in India and to the Curious Draft of the Ganges and Gogra by ... M. Anquetil du Perron. The New Chirographical Map of the Southern Countries of India by Col. Kelly. . . .'

On this map, the Manasarovar Lake in the north is shown about three times larger in size than the nearby lake called Lanka Dhe (Map 4.11.1). Two upper branches of the river Ganges are clearly marked. The northern one is named 'Ganga or the River'. It issues from the western slopes of Mount Kentaisse (Mt. Kailas) and flows westward. At about longitude 75° 30' east, it turns southward, where it meets at about 34° latitude, the southern branch coming from the east, also named on the map as 'Ganga or the River'. This lower 'Ganga' again has two upper branches, not named. The northern one issues from the western range of Mount Kentaisse running almost parallel to the upper, northern 'Ganga', described above. The other branch comes out of the Manasarovar Lake, both meeting at about 80° longitude. Strangely enough, on this part of 'Ganga' on its uzpper course is written, 'the Ganges called here Satlooja (Sutlej) from a supposition it Communicates with river in Penjab'. This shows de la Rochette's confusion about the river Sutlej in this part of the country. Together, these two branches flow westward to meet the upper 'Ganga'. The river, thereafter, is called by de la Rochette as 'Ganges', which then flows southward, cutting through a 'very high snow covered' mountain range, reaching 'Gangotri or the Fall of the Ganges called also the Cow's Mouth'. Still flowing westward till it reaches Bhanceti; turning south-eastward, it comes to Allahabad ; flows onward, forming a large delta after meeting many rivers, like Hooghly, and Brahmaputra, before entering the Bay of Bengal. The map of de la Rochette also shows the route taken by the Lama surveyors sent by the Chinese Emperor in 1711 to explore the 'source of the Ganges' discussed earlier. River 'Sind or Indus or Enidir of the Ancient Hindoos' (Map 4.11.1) issues from a place about 36° latitude and 74° 50' longitude approximate, south of the mountain called 'Mus Tag Snowy Mountain' by the Tatars' or the eastern range of Kuber mountains. It flows in the west-southwest direction in its upper course for about 1° of longitude before it turns south-westward, and then goes on to meet the sea.

The map of de la Rochette also shows the lake 'Chiamay' (Map 4.11.2), in Assam in the

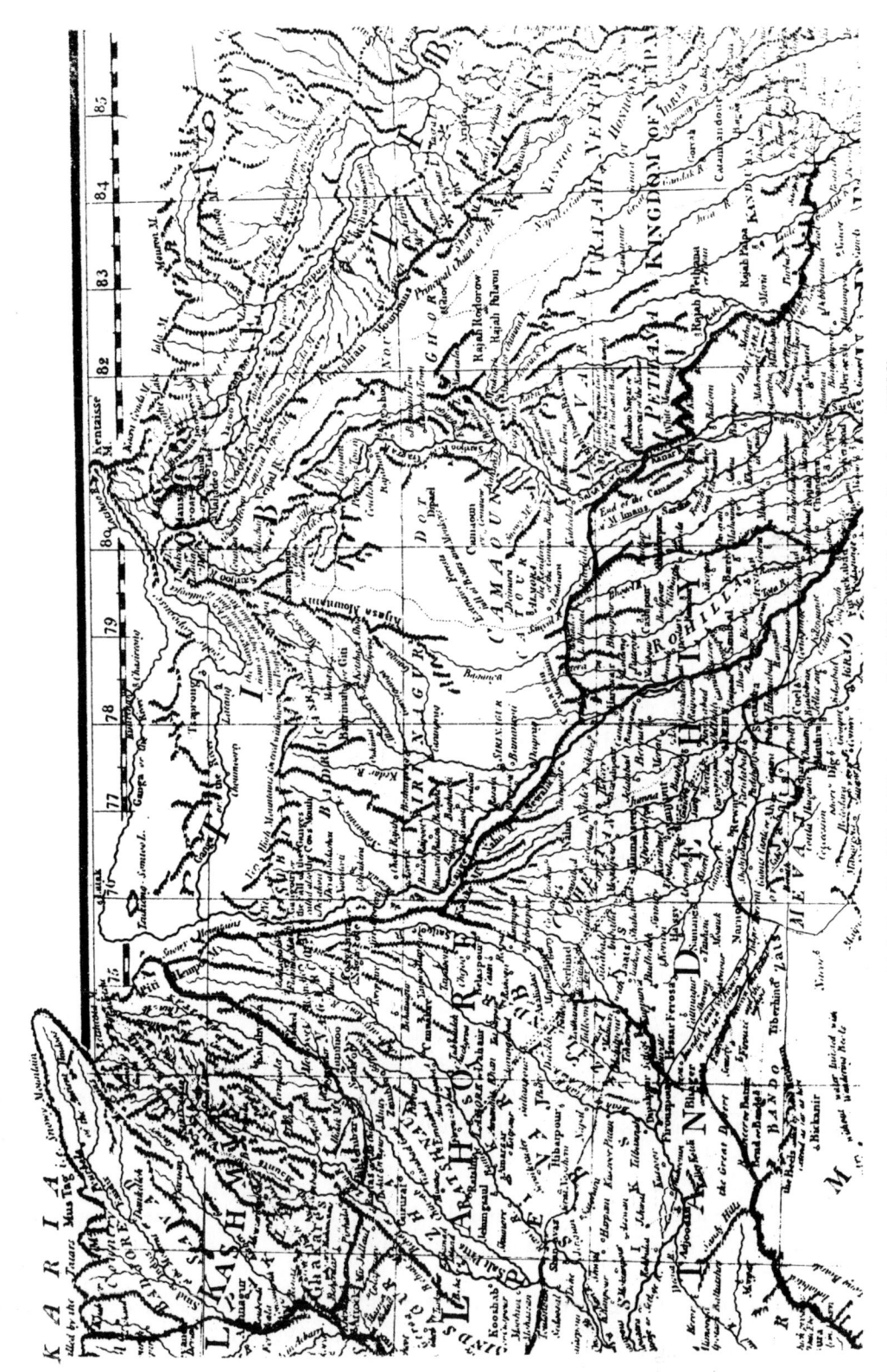

Map 4.11.1: Detail of *Hind, Hindoostan or India* (N) by L.S. de la Rochette (1788).

northeast, below 28° parallel and about 95° longitude. The strange aspect of the lake on this map is that it is shown oval in shape. Two rivers are marked meeting each other inside the lake. The one coming from the north west is drawn in double lines, indicating that it is a broader river, and is named as 'Tsanpoo . . . accord' to Plaisted (one of the earlier surveyors of the British East India Company) 1768 and the Old Maps', and the other river is shown in single line, being a small river, and is named 'Lactoroa R'. They meet in the lower half of the lake. Jointly, they form 'Lakia R. of Plaisted' and flow westward. Later on, still in Assam, they are marked 'Brahmapootren or Brehmapooter R', and still flowing westward. The third river, coming from the north towards the lake at its northeast shore, at its upper course, has a tributary, named 'West Branch'. The main river, in its upper course, is stated, 'Noitsho R. of the Jesuits which communicate with the Kempoo or Arakan R. or with the River of Ava'. Just above the 28° parallel, on the northeast of the lake, it is written, 'Brahmapootren according to the Historian of Aurangzeb'; from that very point, it moves southeast, then southward, almost parallel to the eastern shore of the lake, and then from a place at about 27° latitude, it turns northeast. The whole river is drawn in bold line. But there seems to be some confusion in the mind of de la Rochette about the courses of the main rivers, the 'Tsanpoo' and the 'Brahmpootren', especially in and around the lake. The 'Tsanpoo' River after flowing almost the entire length of the lake, turns south-west just before it, but still inside the lake, its course is shown in double dotted lines, emerging out of the lake in south-east direction and after some distance (marked in double dotted lines) meets the river of Aurangzeb's historian which in this region is called the 'Tsanpoo according to the Jesuits'. This gives the indication that the 'Tsanpoo' River, after emerging from the lake, flows in the south-east direction, and a branch of this river turns westward here forming 'Lakia River'. Since both 'Tsanpoo' inside the lake and then out of it turning westward (Lakia R.) are shown in continuous bold double lines, it appears to be the main river in the lake area.

There seems to be another confusion in this area. River 'Brahmpootren' of Aurangzeb's historian is shown in bold continuous lines, bypassing the lake in its eastern wing, flowing in the south-east direction, but above the 28° latitude. Another conjectural course, shown in double dotted lines, going south-westward, entering the lake, and meeting the 'Tsanpoo' River inside the lake at a point where earlier detailed conjectural course of the 'Tsanpoo' is shown flowing out of the lake in the south-eastern part of it. All that show that de la Rochette was aware of these possibilities, but the decision regarding the proper courses of these rivers are indicated by the continuous bold lines. This indicates that 'Tsanpoo' coming from the north-west, enters the lake and near the southern shore, but still inside the lake, emerges out and flows south-westward into Assam; And 'Brahmapootren' which de la Rochette marks as a separate river, coming from the north, flowing south, bypasses the lake on its eastern shores, and flows down south-eastward.

The above indicates that this map by de la Rôchette is a tremendous departure from the earlier maps being published since many centuries. It shows the awareness of the cartographer about the current geographical trends and their lacunae in the subcontinent during the latter half of the eighteenth century.

Turning towards the 'Ganga' of the Deccan (Map 4.11.3), a very significant and interesting change is visible. Coming out from the eastern slopes of the Western Ghats, to the north-

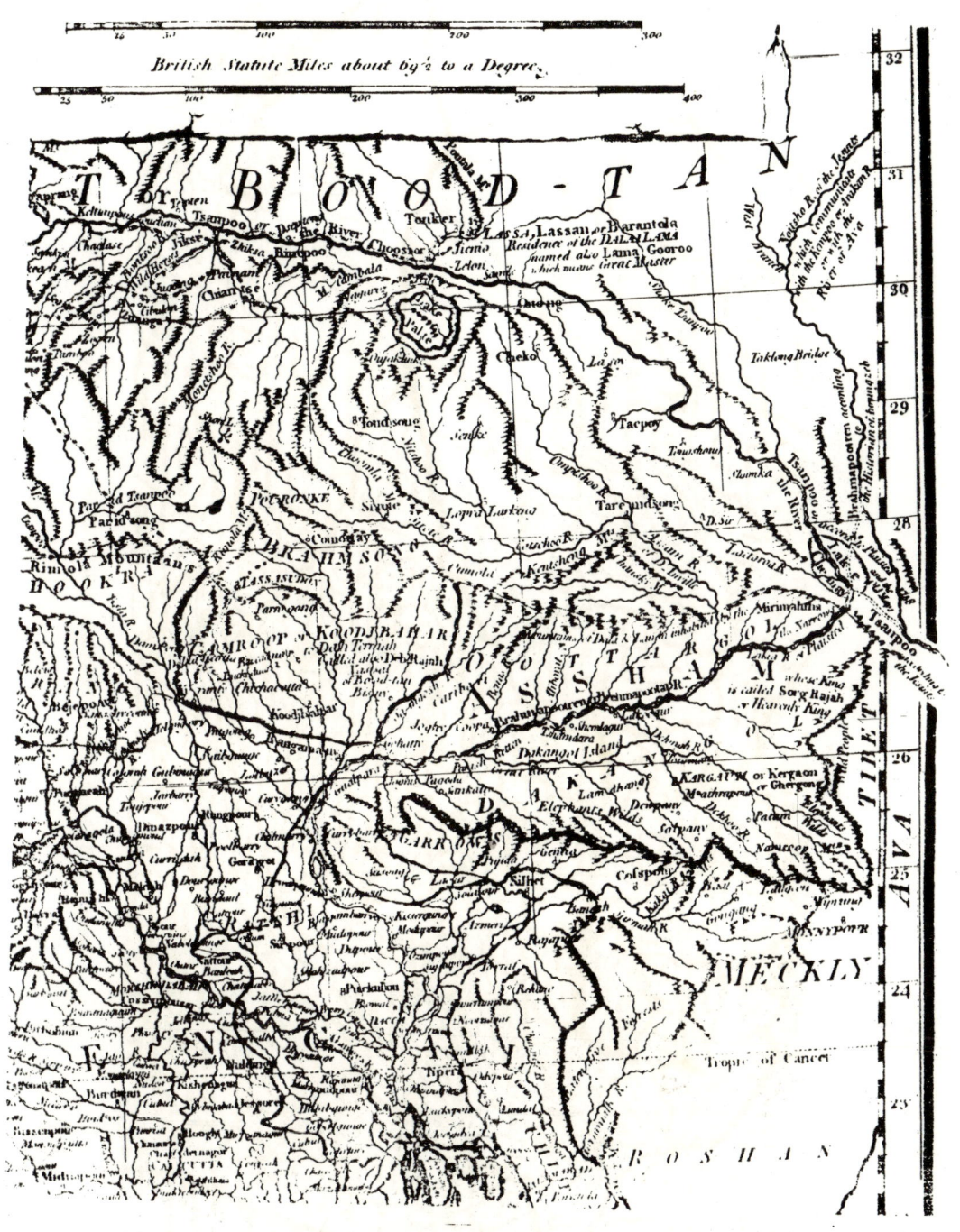

Map 4.11.2: Detail of *Hind, Hindoostan or India* (E) by L.S. de la Rochette (1788).

Map 4.11.3: Detail of *Hind, Hindoostan or India* (S) by L.S. de la Rochette (1788).

west of Daulatabad, while still flowing south of the district, it is called as 'Ganga or Guadavery'. Further down, moving almost eastward at a place about 19°50' latitude, before reaching the northern slopes of 'Tellingana mountains', the river is still named as 'The Ganga called also ...idamy (Not descipherable) and Gaudavery'. Here the river turns its course towards south-eastward, passing through Rajahmundry and it enters the Bay of Bengal. No river, as such, is shown flowing north-eastward in the region, through Berar, which is the normal course of the river 'Ganga' in other earlier maps of the century.

In 1788 itself, James Rennell, while discussing the evidence available to him regarding the source of the Ganges, states:

To sum up the whole information, collected from different accounts of the upper part of the course of the Ganges, it appears that the two branches of it, which spring from the western side of Mt. Kentaisse, take course westward inclining considerably to the north, for a course of about 300 miles, ... when meeting the great chain ... of Mount Himmaleh, which extends from Cabul along the north of Hindoostan, ...the rivers are compelled to turn to the south; in which course they unite their waters, and form, what is properly termed the river Ganges. This body of water now forces a passage *through* the ridge of Mount Himmaleh.... And sapping its very foundation, rushes through a cavern, and precipitates itself into vast bason which it has worn in the rock, at the hither foot of the mountains. ... From this second source ... its course becomes more easterly than before, through the rugged country of Sirinagur (Srinagar); until at Hardwar, it finally escapes from the mountainous tract, in which it has wandered for about 800 B. miles.[44]

This beautiful picture of the upper course of the Ganges is painted by Rennell on receiving information's of Lamas' surveys, referred to earlier, and those of M. Tieffenthaller's travels in the region, The Lamas, as already noted, wrongly showed the upper movement of the Ganges, and added to it was the assertion of Tieffenthaller that he actually visited Gangotri and placed the town of Srinagar *north* of Hardwar. Both these statements, according to Rennell, were utterly wrong, resulting in incorrect delineation of the upper course around the town of Srinagar by Rennell. He corrected his views in the year 1793, while revising his map of Hindoostan. He writes: 'I suspect that the Ganges does not take quite so wide a circuit to the north-west, as is there described ... the place where the Ganges enters the plains of Hindoostan, is placed under the 28° of latitude, though it is known by our late observations to be about 30°.'[45]

Thus, Rennell's observations, regarding the three major fallacies under investigation, were able to tilt the geographical thoughts of the late-eighteenth and early nineteenth centuries of European cartographers and casual map-makers towards proper understanding of Indian geography.

NOTES

1. Susan Gole, *India Within the Ganges*, New Delhi, 1983, p. 64.
2. R.H. Phillimore, *Historical Records of the Survey of India*, vol. I, Dehra Dun, p. 209; Susan Gole, *A Series of Early Printed Maps of India in Facsimile*, New Delhi, 1984, T. 27.

3. Susan Gole, ibid., M. 27(b).
4. Ibid., M. 27(a).
5. Ibid., T. 23-49.
6. Ibid., T. 23.
7. Ibid., T-M. 24.
8. Ibid., T-M. 28-9.
9. Ibid., T-M. 31.
10. Ibid., T-M. 33-4; Lou Sebock (ed.), Public Archives of Canada, National Map Collection, *French Atlases in the Rare Atlas Collection,* Provisional Series, vol. 1, 1974, Introduction, p. 2.
11. Ibid., T-M. 36, 37; Lou Sebock, *French Atlases,* ibid., pp. 1-2.
12. Ibid., T-M. 40, 41.
13. Ibid., T-M. 44.
14. Ibid., T-M. 39, 42-a, 42-b.
15. Ibid., T-M. 45-7.
16. Ibid., T-M. 49.
17. R.H. Phillimore, op. cit., vol. I, pp. 70, 71.
18. Ibid., vol. I, p. 70; Helen Wallis, 'Missionary Cartographers to China', in *Geographical Magazine,* vol. 47, no. 12, London, 1975, pp. 751-9.
19. Clement Markham, *Narrative of the Mission of George Bogle of Tibet,* London, 1879, p. lxi.
20. R.H. Phillimore, op. cit., vol. I, p. 70; S. Noti, *Joseph Tieffentaller, S.J. A Forgotten Geographer of India,* Bombay, 1906, p. 409.
21. Ibid., p. 70; ibid., p. 409.
22. Susan Gole, *A Series.,* op. cit., T-M. 36, 37; Lou Sebock, *French Atlases,* op. cit., pp. 1, 2; R.H. Phillimore, op. cit., vol. I, pp. 210-11.
23. R.H. Phillimore, ibid., vol. I, p. 210.
24. Susan Gole, *A Series,* op. cit., M. 36.
25. R.H. Phillimore, ibid., vol. I, p. 210.
26. Ibid., vol. I, p. 213; James Rennell, *Memoir of a Map of Hindoostan,* 3rd edn., London, 1793, p. vii.
27. Ibid., vol. I, p. 210; William Herbert, *A Geographical Illustration of Map of India,* 1759, p. 39.
28. R.H. Phillimore, op. cit., vol. I, pp. 210-11.
29. Ibid., p. 212; quoted from *Orme MSS,* 33, India Office Library and Records, London, p. 9.
30. Ibid., p. 210; quoted from H.R. Mill, *The Records of the Royal Geographical Society, 1830-1939,* p. 5.
31. Govt. of India, Original Records of Home Dept., Public Consultant A, dt. 22 Dec. 1783.
32. James Rennell, *Memoir.,* op. cit., 1793, p. 366.
33. P.L. Madan, *Indian Cartography, A Historical Perspective,* New Delhi, 1997, pp. 82-3.
34. Susan Gole, *A Series.,* op. cit., T-M. 40, 41.
35. Ibid., T-M. 39, 42(a), 42(b); R.H. Phillimore, op. cit., vol. I, p. 211(n.7).
36. Ibid., T-M. 42(b).
37. Ibid., T-M. 42(b).
38. Ibid., T-M. 42(a).
39. Ibid., T-M. 47.
40. R.H. Phillimore, op. cit., vol. I, p. 213; James Rennell, 'Preface', *Memoir,* 1793.
41. Ibid., p. 213.
42. Ibid., p. 213.
43. Ibid., p. 213.
44. Ibid., p. 73; quoted from James Rennell, *Memoir,* op. cit., 1793, p. 233.
45. James Rennell, *Memoir,* op. cit., 1793, p. 300.

CHAPTER 5

Ultimate Scenario

Culmination of eighteenth-century geographical thought, so far as the history of the controversial aspects of our investigation are concerned, could well be seen in the last map of the century, entitled 'A New Map of Hindoostan',[1] by Thomas Jefferys, published posthumously, in 1794. It may be recalled that he had written a letter in 1768 a letter to the Court of Directors, British East India Company, London, requesting permission to use the geographical material collected by James Rennell in England lying with the Company. The permission, however, came after his death in 1769. The publishers, Laurie & Whittle, deleted his name from the published map,[2] but included therein the information from Rennell's collection, and published it in 1794. This could rightly be called Jefferys' map of 1794.

In this map, the Chiamay Lake was deleted from the region. Since the map does not cover the territory of the origin of the Ganges in the Himalaya, this aspect could be presumed to rest at a place where Rennell put it in his map of 1793, referred earlier; and river 'Ganga' disappeared from the peninsular India for all times to come. The original 'Ganga' of other map-makers took the name 'Godavery' with a different course flowing south-east to meet the Bay of Bengal, for the future cartographers.

From the above, it is evident that during the eighteenth century, the upper course of the so-called 'eastern boundary' of India of the antiquity, the river Ganges, received ample attention from serious cartographers and map-makers like Chatelain (Map 21), D'Anville (Map 26), Vaugondy (Maps 28.1-28.3), Jefferys (Maps 30.1-30.3), de la Rochette (Maps. 32.1-32.3), and others mentioned, Rennell's assertions, contrary to the views expressed by most of the map-makers, came quite late in the century. But still, the credibility of these cartographers was never in doubt. Chatelain was known for his practice of combining map and text; his many text volumes carried all about the maps 'necessary for a well-read gentleman at the Court';[3] Jefferys was the 'Geographer to the King of England';[4] D'Anville was the official cartographer for the French East India Company;[5] de la Rochette was known for his serious attitude towards the subject. But somehow, as the history of the controversies indicate, all the map-makers were tempted to show the glaring geographical fallacies in their maps. Some, however, expressed their dissent, but much later in the eighteenth and early nineteenth centuries in a mild way, even when following the 'crowd'. Why this was so is not comprehensible easily, and one can only surmise.

To recapitulate—there were three prominent inaccuracies that dominated the Indian segment for centuries since the later years of the BC era. Their circulation received a boost in the Middle Ages when Latin literature with its fancy for myths, fables, and fantasies, both literary and geographical, was in vogue. The hold of Christianity over the world of geographical thought and speculation, was, apparently, not slackening. These fallacies reached the point of absurdity and mystified the cartographers and map-makers when the so-called 'travel accounts'; or 'eye-witness accounts' were in great demand in the West.

The first, the geographically controversy centred around the source of India's holiest and most venerated of the rivers, the Ganges. This river again came up on the geographical horizon late in the BC era, when it first peeped in the geographical controversial scenario, since its emergence more than a millennium years ago. The controversy heated up with Ptolemy's thesis on map making in second century AD, and the compilation of his *Geographia* and *Cosmographia*. They gave rise to confusion and speculations about the place of the origin of the Ganges at a time when the distinction between 'diagrammatic or graphic representations' of the earth-form of the world and the 'geographical map' became apparent and almost accepted by the geographers and the map-makers of the time. The controversy was resurrected from time to time by the interesting details that came up in the print-media about the place of origin of the Ganges, like the one by the Persian historian of Scereseddin Timur, who, in the fifteenth century reached up to the 'entrance of the Strait of Kupela', the supposed area of the Ganga's origin. Father Monserrate speculated it in 1590; Mughal Emperor Akbar sent a fact-finding mission in the late sixteenth century to the holy place; William Baffin's depiction of it in his well-known map of India of 1619; fantastic and highly imaginative map of Asia in 1637 by none other than the grandson of Gerar Mercator, the world famous cartographer, Rumold Mercator; the writings of Edward Terry, the Chaplain to Sir Thomas Roe in 1655 after his visit to the 'source' of the river Ganges in 1612; and the subsequent publications of maps during the long period of this century showing the 'source' in the rugged and mighty Himalaya, and the further course of the Ganges by many famous and reputed cartographers, and the writers of 'travel accounts' which deluged European readers.

The origin of the second fallacy, we know, was the reporting of the mythical lake 'Chiamay' in the far north-east of Assam by Marco Polo in the thirteenth century, and further confirmation of its existence by Mendes Pinto in 1614, but calling it as lake 'Singapamor', the supposed place of the source of the rivers like Ganges and Brahmaputra by many map-makers; and the subsequent depiction of the lake on their maps by well-known and respected map-makers and cartographers for centuries.

The mid-sixteenth century was the period when the third fallacy came on the cartographic scenario. It crept in when de Barros published his famous work Decadas in 1552. The narrative was illustrated with maps wherein he described a large river named 'Ganga' in peninsular India, when there was none by that name and description existing in the region. Coming from such a credible pen, this blunder was quoted and copied for centuries, none bothering to counter-check. All the map-makers were tempted to carry on the glaring geographical fallacies in their maps in spite of empirical data being available; 'close-by', but they didn't 'lift their hands to pick it up' for a long time.

The confusion regarding the origin of the venerated, holy river Ganges; the 'mesmerizing' lake in the north-eastern Assam—the supposed birthplace of many rivers like the Ganges, the Brahmaputra of some map-makers since early historic times; and the lure of peninsular

'Ganga' of the credible, imaginative, speculative, and artistic cartographers and map-makers of the last few centuries are now no more. These have given place to dreary and monotonous, though crystal clear vista created by machines, mathematicians, and the carto-scientists of modern age.

NOTES

1. Susan Gole, *A Series of Early Printed Maps of India in Facsimile*, New Delhi, 1984, T-M. 42(b).
2. Ibid., T-M. 42(b).
3. Ibid., T-M. 28.
4. Ibid., T. 39.
5. Ibid., T. 36; Lou Sebock, *Atlases Published in the Netherlands in the Rare Atlas Collections*, Provincial Series, No. 1, Ottawa, 1974, Introduction, pp. i, ii.

Postscript

Following the publication of Jefferys' map of 1794, the lake 'Chaimay' was no more to be seen on the subsequent maps of the region. From the academic point of view, it may be mentioned that Brahmakund, a place south of Lohitpur in east Assam, was discovered in 1826.[1] Its present reference is, 'Standard Sheet of India', No. 92 A/5.

It is not a lake but a small town on the southern banks of Brahmaputra river, the place where the river is very wide, with many islands in the river bed, giving the impression of a large lake.

★ ★ ★

The English and the European powers, especially the French, through their army surveyors, were regularly gathering topographical information on the territories of their operations, or the region through which their armies marched. By the end of the eighteenth century, their armies had traversed the region through which the river 'Ganga' of peninsular India was shown by the map-makers for centuries. As noted earlier, the coastal area of Orissa was surveyed in detail in the latter half of the eighteenth century by many British surveyors.[2] Their reports, traverse records and charts do not show such a river in the area or it falling into the Bay of Bengal. After this, the existence of the river 'Ganga' in the Deccan was disapproved by the cartographers.

★ ★ ★

In the early years of the nineteenth century, in 1810 to be precise,[3] the source of the Ganges was surveyed by W.S. Webb, an English surveyor. He had made extensive surveys of the river Ganges, mostly in the plains, earlier around 1800.[4] Others like Henry Huygens, J.N. Rind, R.H. Colebrook, Robert Knox, F.S. White, Stephen, J.B. Fraser, J.A. Hodgson, J.D. Herbert, P.W. Grant, in their official and semi-official capacities as surveyors of the British East India Company, were involved in unveiling the mysteries of the river Ganges between 1766 and 1820, especially the origin and its course in the plains.

Thus ended the long quest, for the 'eastern boundary of India' and the fallacies and inaccuracies connected with the course of the Ganges. Consequent to the efforts of the geographers and map-makers, speculations about the origin and the upper course of the 'mysterious' river, and its mythical incarnations in the peninsular India, since the evolution of the early Mesopotamian, Egyptian, Greek and the Western civilizations, were successfully concluded.

NOTES

1. *Asiatic Researches*, vol. XIV, 1822, pp. 436-7.
2. Govt. of India, Original Records of Home Dept., Public Consultation A, dt. 22 Dec. 1783.
3. S.N. Prasad (ed.), *Catalogue of the Historical Maps of the Survey of India, 1700-1900*, New Delhi, 1975, folio 15/7.
4. Ibid., folios 10, 13, 15, 17, 101, 168, 170, etc.

Epilogue

To the early Western world, India was a land of monsters, mystics, myths, and fables, lying far away somewhere in the East. Many of these ideas were enmeshed in European popular imagination, and subsequently, through the Middle Ages and the Crusading Era, these gradually penetrated popular literature, including Latin. Many of these were even 'Christianized'.

In the great epics *Ramayana and Mahabharata*, and in the voluminous literature of the *Puranas*, abundant myths and legends are wound around the sanctity of the Ganges.[1] Geographically speaking, the Ganges rises at 30° 55' N, 79° 7' E approximately. At its origin, it is called Bhagirathi which comes out from an ice-cave near Gangotri; later it meets Jahanavi coming from the north-east, and then river Alaknanda. The united stream then finally out of the Himalayas and becomes the Ganges.[2]

Not only the Ganges, but other rivers in India too have an element of sanctity attached to them from a supposed connection with the waters of the Ganges or 'Ganga'[3] since time immemorial. The river Ganges is devotedly called '*Ganga Maiya*', or '*Ganga Maa*' (Mother Ganges). Veneration for the river still figures in the modern age as the chief article in the creed of modern Hinduism.[4]

★   ★   ★

No less venerated is another river called Wainganga which literally means 'the arrow of water' (of the Ganges). This river rises near the village of Partabpur or Mudara (21°57'N, and 79°34'E), and is about 11 miles from the town of Seoni in Madhya Pradesh.

The legend goes that a king of Bhandara, in Maharashtra, was a very devout Hindu. He used to bathe daily in the river Ganges before beginning his daily routine. This was possible because he possessed a *Tilasman*. By placing it in his mouth, he could deport to Allahabad, the *Sangam*, the confluence of the Ganges and the Jumna rivers. After bathing in the Ganges, he used to return back to his native place. This ritual went on for many years without interruption. When he became very old, the 'mother Ganga' one day told him to collect some of her water in a container and take it to his native place and put the container near his house. At once, there would spring up a stream from the place. Its water would also be that of the Ganges and have the same divine properties, and by bathing in it, he would have the same religious efficacy. The king was very much pleased. As destined, on his return journey, he felt very tired and stopped to rest at Partabpur village, the present source of Wainganga. As soon as he, inadvertently, placed the container on the ground, a spring of pure water sprang up from the place and began to flow northward. Realizing his mistake, he besought the Ganges to stop the flow as he was still far away from his house and would not be in a position to come there daily. At this, the river changed its course, and taking a turn north-eastward, began flowing south in wide semi-circle until it passed through Bhandara by the king's house.[5]

★ ★ ★

The main tributary of Wainganga is Penganga. This river rises from south of Ajanta hills of the Western Ghats, about 15 km west of the town of Buldana district in present Maharashtra. It meets the Wardha river about 15 km (about 19°52'N, and 79°10'E) west of Chandrapur district, also in Maharashtra, which finally meets Wainganga near Chaprata (19°55'N, 79°50'E) in the district of the same name, and flows almost southward under the name of Pranhita, which finally meets Godavari near Sironcha at about (18°50'N, 79°57'E).[6] Development of the Godavari has already been discussed while analysing the maps of G.R. de Vaugondy (1688-1766), Thomas Jefferys (d. 1771), and L. S. de la Rochette (active in 1788), in the latter half of the eighteenth century.[7]

★ ★ ★

Is there any connection discerned with the Deccan 'Ganga'? If so, it took centuries for the Western cartographers to come to realities. WHY?

NOTES

1. *Imperial Gazeteer of India*, 1908, vol. XII, p. 134.
2. Ibid., vol. XII, p. 132.
3. Ibid., 1881, vol. III, p. 292.
4. Ibid., vol. III, p. 292.
5. Ibid., 1908, vol. XXII, pp. 349-50.
6. See the last chapter.
7. Ibid.

Bibliography

Asiatic Researches, vol. XIV, 1822.
Atlas of Ancient Classical Geography, London: J.M. Dent Sons Ltd., 1952.
Bagrow, Leo, *History of Cartography* (Eng. edn.), revised and enlarged by R.K. Skelton, London, 1964.
Beazley, C.R., *The Dawn of Modern Geography*, London, 1897.
Cary, M. and E.H. Warmington, *The Ancient Explorers*, London, 1929.
East and West, vol. V, January-June 1906.
Gole, Susan, *Early Maps of India*, New Delhi, 1976.
———, *India Within the Ganges*, New Delhi, 1983.
———, *A Series of Early Printed Maps of India in Facsimile*, New Delhi, 1984.
Herbert, William, *A Geographical Illustration of the Map of India*, 1759.
Imperial Gazetteer of India, Calcutta, 1881, 1908.
India, Govt. of, Original Records of Home Dept., Public Consultations, 1783.
Jacob, J., *Barlaam and Josaphat*, London, 1896.
Keith, A. Berriedale, *A History of Sanskrit Literature*, Oxford, 1928.
Kalota, N.S., *India as Described by Megasthenes*, Delhi, 1978.
Lach, Donald F., *Asia in the Making of Europe*, 3 vols., Chicago and London, 1965-93.
Madan, P.L., *Indian Cartography, A Historical Perspective*, New Delhi, 1997.
Markham, Clement R., *Memoir on the Indian Surveys*, 2nd edn., London, 1878.
———, *Narrative of the Mission of George Bogle of Tibet*, London, 1879.
Markham, C., *Book of Knowledge of All the Kingdoms, Lands and Lordships in the World*, London, 1912.
Mascarenhas, Mira, 'The Church in Eighteenth Century Goa', in Testonio R. de Souza (ed.), *Essays in Goan History*, New Delhi, 1989.
McCrindle, J.W., *Ancient India as Described in Classical Literature*, Westminster, 1901.
Mill, H.R., *Records of the Royal Geographical Society, 1830-1930*, London, 1930.
Misra, R.P., *Fundamentals of Cartography*, Mysore, 1969.
Mukherjee, R.K., *A History of Indian Shipping*, 2nd edn., Bombay, 1957.
Noti, S., Joseph Tieffentaller, S.J., *A Forgotten Geographer of India*, Bombay, 1906.
Parry, J.H., *The Age of Reconnaissance*, London, 1963.
Phillimore, R.H., *Historical Records of the Survey of India*, 5 vols., Dehra Dun, vol. I, 1945.
Prasad, S.N. (ed.), *Catalogue of the Historical Maps of the Survey of India, 1700-1900*, New Delhi, 1975.

Ratus, L. (ed.), *Catholic India*, New Delhi, 1982.

Rennell, James, *Memoir of a Map of Hindoostan*, 3rd edn., London, 1793.

Rogers, Francis M., *The Travels of the Infante Dom Pedro of Portugal*, Massachusetts, 1961.

Scott, John A. (revised by L. Olschki), *Marco Polo's Asia: An Introduction to His "Description of the World" Called "Il Milione"*, Berkeley, 1960.

Sebock, Lou (ed.), Public Archives of Canada, National Map Collection, *Atlases Published in the Netherlands in the Rare Atlas Collection*, Provisional Series, no. 1, Ottawa, Canada, 1973.

——— (ed.), *French Atlases in the Rare Atlas Collection*, Provisional Series, vol. 1, Ottawa: Public Archives of Canada, National Map Collection, Canada, 1974.

Thomson, James Oliver, *History of Ancient Geography*, Cambridge, 1948.

Tooley, R.V., *Map and Map-Makers*, London, 1970.

Verlinden, Charles, 'The Indian Ocean: The Ancient Period and the Middle Ages', in Satish Chandra (ed.), *The Indian Ocean Explorations in History, Commerce and Politics*, New Delhi, 1987.

Wellis, Helen, 'Missionary Cartographers to China', in *Geographical Magazine*, vol. 47, no. 12, London, 1975.

Wheatley, Paul, *The Golden Khersonese: Studies in the Historical Geography of the Malay Peninsula before A.D. 1500*, Kuala Lumpur, 1961.